I0450537

# The Ferguson Chronicles:

## August-December 2014
## Real Time Coverage:
### Photos: Tweets, Press Discussions And Live Links

By

## Lonnie Hicks

**ISBN-978-1505671551**

**ISBN-10: 1505671558**

Before we start I might recommend that you take a look at my "Let's Talk About Race: What are the Facts." on this site at:

http://www.authorsden.com/visit/viewshortstory.asp?id=61331&authorid=121255

It takes a look at race and discrimination in an historical context and goes into these issues across thousands of years.

But now in this article to become a book I take the Ferguson situation as a current example.

First let's have look at examples of the press coverage.

**Racism as A Tax and Profit Center and Feeding Off The Poor.**

The Ferguson city budget: Note the increase in traffic fines revenue: up 23% over three years, more than any other item in the budget except capital. Why?

http://www.thedailybeast.com/articles/2014/08/22/ferguson-s-shameful-legal-shakedown-three-warrants-a-year-per-household.html

http://www.fergusoncity.com/DocumentCenter/View/1609

http://www.reuters.com/article/2014/08/19/us-usa-missouri-shooting-tickets-insight-idUSKBN0GJ2CB20140819

Profiting from crime

http://www.alternet.org/speakeasy/chaunceydevega/profits-racism-coward-darren-wilson-who-killed-michael-brown-has-now-raised?paging=off&current_page=1

## Imagine Life As A Poor Person: White or Black

You get up in the morning and you have no job, can't get one because you had a traffic warrant, were stopped and frisked, it went to warrant, you could not pay the fine, and went to jail: spent time, got out and now can't vote, and can't get a job.

You have to shop in stores (if you can find one close to you) that overcharges you for inferior goods at prices above what whites nearby pay for the same goods. That hurts your, slim or non-existent, budget.

You pay higher rent on your apartment which is not maintained by the local slumlord because he/she can get away with it. You got rats, black mold, peeling wall paper, bad toilets and nobody does anything; and you are told "you people live like animals."

Your kids go to schools which are sub-standard and under-funded by even with the property taxes you pay, much of that goes to white schools and do not return to your district to benefit your schools. This means no computers, substitute teachers, low reading, math and SAT scores and unsuccessful college applications.

## So What Is Your Day Like?

You send your kids off to school in the morning where drug dealers await them on the corners and you wonder where are they getting the money to buy the drugs to sell to your kids. People in the ghetto don't have the money to finance huge drugs deals and get to get the drugs to the ghetto. You wonder why the police don't stop your community from being flooded by these cheap drugs, wonder why they don't stop looters but can stop peaceful protesters, can't stop the local city council from zoning in and making possible a liquor store on every corner in your neighbor, but this doesn't happen in white neighborhoods, wonder and marvel that in these stop and frisk situations the police take your bag of grass and use it to plant on the next stop and frisk person, or sell it to make money for themselves, and above all, you realize the cops want to see high crime rates high and looting for television because it means more overtime for themselves and bigger police budgets and medals for stopping "crime."

You kid goes out the door to a sub-standard school where there are state mandated vaccinations and you are aware blacks have been used as guinea pigs over the years and you know birth defects in your community are higher than other communities. And, you have to let your children eat the "free" lunches because you can't afford to feed them sometimes and you wonder what is in the food and you know that school lunch and food stamp programs are profit centers administered by Chase Bank.

http://poorrichardsnews.com/post/65411347291/corporate-welfare-jp-morgan-chase-has-made

High confidence there.

You see your kids exposed to untreated mental health cases because the state facilities have all been closed. Your elderly can't go to nursing homes because the price is too high: you see doctors give up on your grandmother and she dies where she should have lived, perhaps, because black life is not valued. You can't get a car loan at a reasonable interest rate because of warrants and redlining; ditto on credit cards, and if you or someone you love dies, you can't even afford the funeral and often can't even get the body, because doctors and the police don't want autopsies done because they could be sued over what they have done or not done.

Have I mentioned the polluted environment and neighborhoods, you have to live in, next to refineries, dumps, toxic and city?

Unmarried you pay higher state and local taxes than married whites do.

You pay a higher proportion of your income in a retrograde sales tax structure and property taxes where your home equity is degraded because of many of these factors where your neighborhood has been redlined scaring whites into flight--a fact that only benefits real estate agents and the banks- who make a killing on this turnover-at your expense.

You pay more for car insurance, if you can get it, based on your zip code, traffic fines and warrants, so even driving to a job interview can be risky and expensive, especially since the cops have booked you and are now on the look-out for you. Spotting you they can make up any excuse for stopping you, they frisk, search etc. and the merry go around begins again.

Now the justice system and the cops run on this revenue, not to mention the attorneys, yours or the court-appointed one, blood with-drawers, etc. all of this is fed on the backs of the poor; people's jobs depend upon a steady stream of this revenue, and the cops know it. They have quotas on stops. Yes they do.

Did I mention driving schools, the DMV itself feeds on you as well?

Here is an example from Missouri webpage.

http://www.dmv.org/mo-missouri/traffic-tickets.php#Insurance-Rate-Increases

Most likely you end up homeless, living at mom's house, or five to an apartment. You see your sister, aunt or even your own mother prostitute to help pay the bills. It is organized, enforced degradation; a race tax.

**Media Pile-On**
On TV you see yourself 99% of the time portrayed as a drug dealer, dangerous, and preying upon whites, poor, jobless, where why that should be so is never discussed or elucidated.

More importantly, how all this is enforced daily is never discussed or illuminated, until at some point you start to believe this media propaganda yourself. And when your kid asks you "why do they hate us so?" You don't have an answer.

http://www.dailymail.co.uk/news/article-2722613/African-Americans-Twitter-protest-media-s-portrayal-black-people-wake-police-killing-teenager-Michael-Brown-iftheygunnedmedown-hashtag.html

Meantime, White Life is all valley girls, prom dresses, "orange is the new black" and vacations in Greece.

You try for medical care but that is difficult so you end up with unattended to health problems, see friends and relatives dying young, from police bullets or those very same health problems, and you get bitter.

If you or your son or daughter does find a job it is a McDonald's job and pays very little.

There are no unions to help you get ahead in life.

The national government does little to help and even when federal funds come in they go the police department in tanks and guns, and even funds earmarked for the poor are skimmed by the city and state and the money is largely used to get themselves re-elected and to provide jobs for their relatives and friends. Highway funds and jobs only go to whites, ditto for school fundings, you name it.

Try to vote them out and you face voter suppression schemes which are increasingly endorsed by the Supreme Court of the United States. Now even local elections have huge amounts of outside money coming in especially for candidates running for local justice and judicial posts.

The police, the police, are there every day, like an occupying army. Standing outside your own house you are told to move on, or get down on the sidewalk, and if you dare question the officer you are charged with resisting arrest, and now another series of warrants and perhaps back to jail, because you can't pay the heavy fines. You don't have the money for a lawyer to help and court appointed attorneys work for the prosecutor.

Then you find out the city has spent thousands on surveillance equipment, a lot of it in your neighborhood to "fight crime" but is really part of a traffic "spy for cash" program where a city like Ferguson makes 2.6 million dollars a year doing this, the second largest source of income increase in their budget, all this is paying for white cops and "civil servants" that don't live in your neighborhood and are, for you an occupying army, if you protest, they dominate the so-called justice system where a cop is seldom indicted, or charged for murdering black men, children and women.

These stop and frisk programs have proven to be ineffective in reducing crime and mostly benefit the police in terms of scaring citizens in increasing their budgets and their armor and guns, not to mention overtime. Yes, over time is where many police department folks make their money. This is a perverse incentive.

Stop and Frisk Not effective in NY city:

http://rt.com/usa/181976-stop-frisk-ineffective-guns/

On top of it all these cops are paid for by your taxes because the majority of property taxes in Ferguson are paid for by its black residents.

Then, if you protest, you are called "an animal" and besieged by tanks, tear gas and the national guard, (which you also pay for with your taxes.)

If, by some miracle, you overcome all these obstacles, and you graduate from high school, you find that college is not affordable, even if you could find one that would take you, you have to take on thousands of dollars in debt because your mom and dad took on sub-prime debt to get you to that point and Wall Street took the house they had paid for years, back. Gone. Scammed; often forced into bankruptucy.

The City you live in has also been scammed by Wall Street and mom or dads, pensions will not be paid out as planned; that even their savings over the last ten years has earned only 1% percent interest, wall street, literally stole the money.

Even if you get through college and by some miracle you graduate you can't get a job when you get out, except maybe at McDonald's which is threatening to put in robot cooks if you try to unionize.

You and your family, if you have one, has to live on 75$ a week.

"Don't mess with me now because I am close to the edge" to paraphrase the song.

Meantime, white racists cruise the streets carrying arms, threatening, seeming crazy for a racist war to pump bullets into you and yours, and you complain to your local officials and they do nothing.

Ferguson cop speaks out "rabid dog" comment

http://rt.com/usa/182284-police-ferguson-insult-protesters/

http://rt.com/usa/181924-ferguson-officer-kill-protesters/

http://www.truth-out.org/opinion/item/26063-time-to-get-rid-of-racist-policing-in-the-united-states

New video of killing a second black man

http://rt.com/usa/181772-deadly-st-louis-shooting-video/

Under the stress you feel bad about not being able to support your family, even date a girl, because you don't have the money, a car, or a job, you decide to sell some pot just to feed the family, help with stress, and they stop and frisk you and give you 15 years.

You sit in stir and think about the fact that whites don't even know about all this, yet benefit from this system, and don't want to know about it and if you complain in prison, it is 10 years of solitary confinement.

All through this you are told to pray, don't go to violence, be patient and call your congressman.

This new Jim Crow in America, this is slow genocide, and Americakkk.

This is how you feel.

Angry? Yeah. Angry.

**12 Things White People And Others Can Do About Ferguson**

Few in the white tribe will speak out fearing retribution from other members of the white tribe family or friends. If you don't think so check out face book entries on this topic.

Here one that did speak out.

http://www.nationofchange.org/justice-ginsburg-america-has-real-racial-problem-1408803839

**Months later what happens to the cop who did the shooting?**

http://www.alternet.org/civil-liberties/heres-what-happens-police-officers-who-shoot-unarmed-black-men

Then if you starting reading you find out that it is indeed not just a one city problem but a country-wide pattern and fits into a global pattern. You start to realize that it is a global system that is being built and is a coordinated one.

**Red Light Camera World Wide**- Making cameras and the law pay. Increasing taxes and revenue the traffic way.

http://en.wikipedia.org/wiki/Red_light_camera

Who is running this locally and worldwide?

See:

http://www.authorsden.com/visit/viewshortstory.asp?id=59847&authorid=121255

http://www.alternet.org/economy/how-ultra-rich-01-have-sucked-even-more-americas-wealth-you-think?akid=12158.260128.WpCMfl&rd=1&src=newsletter1016531&t=4

Allan Watt

https://www.youtube.com/watch?feature=player_detailpage&v=GArlDpwvFhc


**Mega-Bucks Traffic Fines and Revenue For Cities**

http://www.slate.com/blogs/moneybox/2014/08/18/ferguson_police_department_the_economic_incentives_that_make_cops_harass.html

http://www.avvo.com/legal-guides/ugc/are-cities-agressively-looking--at-traffic-fines-for-revenue

http://www.foxbusiness.com/personal-finance/2011/10/19/town-that-lived-off-speeding-tickets/

http://www.foxnews.com/story/2009/02/10/speeding-parking-tickets-on-rise-as-government-revenue-source/

**The Fort Worth Example:**

"In the Fort Worth area alone, roughly 400,000 of tickets are issued for Class C misdemeanors, traffic violations and parking citations annually. Recent data shows that nearly 850,000 tickets were handed out since January of 2008, and 125,000 of them resulted in the issuance of bench warrants. Considering the amount of uncollected fees, fines and court costs associated with those unpaid tickets and the warrants themselves, the city is waiting on nearly $80 million of payments. The situation is almost as dire in nearby Arlington; that city has over 100,000 active warrants stemming from unpaid citations. The economic impact of non-payment of these bills extends beyond the city governments themselves; the state of Texas receives a portion of all recovered fees, so they are adding fuel to the fire, pressing cities to make more aggressive collection efforts."

From:

http://www.avvo.com/legal-guides/ugc/are-cities-agressively-looking--at-traffic-fines-for-revenue

http://www.diversityinc.com/news/history-racially-charged-violence/

8/23/14

6.2 billion in speeding ticket as of 7/14? Is this a racket? This does not even count warrants, fines and the rest. Feed off the poor and now the middle class and the out-of-town driver.

**The System Is Predatory And Parasitic Against The Poor, And Makes Money Off Their Poverty**.

http://www.statisticbrain.com/driving-citation-statistics/

"Many of the protesters described their frustrations with a system that locks people up for unpaid parking tickets. Despite having just over 21,000 residents, Ferguson issued over 32,000 arrest warrants for non-violent offenses — most of them driving violations — in 2013."

From:

http://www.huffingtonpost.com/2014/08/28/in-ferguson-a-sense-of-no_n_5732502.html

8/26/14

**More on the Probation Spiral And Civil Forfeiture**

After the warrants comes the probation spiral. Once in the system the justice system wants to keep you there.

The rules are:

1. One mistake and more fines. Five minutes late and they lock the court room doors and you can't get in and get "a failure to appear" and another warrant and more fines. You have trouble getting there, it is often at a place you don't know, their paper work requires faxing, a computer, a home printer, Wi-Fi and you don't have ready access to these; all this designed to trip you up.

There is endless paperwork because so many agencies want to get their share of the loot; from judges, police, probation, social work, prison, DMV, attorneys, prosecutors, court-appointed attorneys, lots and lots of people live off those fines.

2. Break any of the myriad rules and the same: more fines; probation officer etc. all designed to keep you in the system because the ultimate goal is jail. destruction of the individual, of family and jobs for the justice system people. This happens all over America and in most the West as well.

3. On probation, if you get stopped, the cops have the right to confiscate, repeat confiscate your car, your goods, anything they can get their hands on. Repeat: anything, which they sell to get money for their own salaries.

4. If you can't pay you go to jail. This is, in effect, the re-creation of debtor prisons. The poor today; the middle class tomorrow.

Not in America you say?

Take a look:
Debtor Imprisonment in the United States

https://www.aclu.org/blog/tag/debtors-prisons

http://www.foxnews.com/politics/2013/12/28/local-courts-reviving-debtors-prison-for-overdue-fines-fees/

"Advocates are trying to convince courts that aside from the legal questions surrounding the practice, it is disproportionately jailing poor people and doesn't even boost government revenues -- in fact, governments lose money in the process.

"It's a waste of taxpayer resources, and it undermines the integrity of the justice system," Carl Takei, staff attorney for the ACLU's National Prison Project, told FoxNews.com.

"The problem is it's not actually much of a money-making proposition ... to throw people in jail for fines and fees when they can't afford it. If counties weren't spending the money jailing people for not paying debts, they could be spending the money in other ways."

The Brennan Center for Justice at New York University's School of Law released a"

Tool Kit for Action

"in 2012 that broke down the cost to municipalities to jail debtors in comparison with the amount of old debt it was collecting. It doesn't look like a bargain. For example, according to the report, Mecklenburg County, N.C., collected $33,476 in debts in 2009, but spent $40,000 jailing 246 debtors -- a loss of $6,524"

What the writer doesn't understand is that the payoff in Ohio at least goes under the table to judges, in the famous "cash for kids" scandals in that state. Who was paying off the judges, the private prison system because they make money by filling those jail beds?

Probation Profiling

http://www.ktvu.com/videos/news/profiling-for-dui-offenders/vCpyNH/

See: The Scandal of Civil Forfeiture

http://www.authorsden.com/visit/viewshortstory.asp?id=59408&authorid=121255

The Impounding Scam

http://ay.gy/rVEIo

"When events like the Michael Brown shooting occur that inflame people and motivate them to take to the streets to protest, we are reminded that there is not justice for all in America. We must also acknowledge and condemn the daily injustices born of a system that slowly grinds down the people who can least afford it, and, in too many cases to count, leads to their early death. In the line at the San Francisco impound lot; I overheard the crying woman ahead of me telling the clerk, "I need my car to get home to my children." The clerk responded, "I wish I could help you, ma'am, but if you don't have the money, there's nothing I can do."

Impounding: A Nation-Wide Money-Maker for Cities?

http://www.wave3.com/story/12773921/city-revenue-from-towing-cars-skyrockets

http://www.nbclosangeles.com/news/local/Car-Impounds-to-Be-Debated-140715003.html

http://www.ktvu.com/videos/news/profiling-for-dui-offenders/vCpyNH/

If a white person tries to help you, and is riding in the same car, it is a guarantee you will be pulled over. Discipline of whites social and legal is common, a warning to them not to help you or be seen with you.

If you drive in a white neighborhood you are a target; period. On the freeways passing white areas, at night, cops shine lights into the cars to spot black drivers, to intimidate them into never coming back that way again. To be seen in a white neighborhood is to be stopped and intimidated or worse.

The sad fact is that most blacks never leave their neighborhoods and seldom travel more than 25 miles from their home. There is a reason for that. So they are trapped in their neighborhoods, no car, and grocery owners know this and charge them more. That is why there is so much animosity against immigrant store owners because their prices are higher and this is not just because they are small (see dollar stores) it is because you sooner or later sense the exploitation immobility allows.

If you get a car, a nice car, you immediately become a target, suspected of having stolen it. The truth is that country- wide 95% of all these stops produce no evidence of crime, that is if the local police force keeps statistics and if they do, those statistics cannot be trusted.

Whites are constantly in the press, being propagandized so they fall silent at injustices, thinking, "it is probably true and/or simply afraid to speak out, because of hatred coming their way from their own white tribe. But many depend upon that the income from all of this and don't want to speak out against their own interests.

What a country.

Trying escape all this by joining the military is not a solution. You get put in harm's way as matter of course, and are asked to go off overseas and kill Asians, Iraqis, or whomever, to bring to them the benefits of Democracy.

What a country,

8/25/14

**John Oliver Video on Ferguson**

http://www.vox.com/xpress/2014/8/18/6030265/john-oliver-ferguson-monologue

Daily Show on Ferguson

http://thedailyshow.cc.com/videos/ufqeuz/race-off

]
Next we do:

Gentrification, Politics and Leadership and the Prison Industrial Complex

Meantime see:

http://www.newyorker.com/magazine/2014/06/23/get-out-of-jail-inc

http://www.truth-out.org/buzzflash/commentary/the-us-incarceration-system-ruins-the-lives-of-the-poor-

and-favors-the-wealthy

Celebrities and Ferguson who has spoken out and who took the ice bucket challenged?

http://www.huffingtonpost.com/2014/08/19/middlebrow-ferguson-ice-bucket_n_5692645.html

**A Compendium of Coverage**

http://ibw21.org/ferguson/

http://www.kpfa.org/archive/id/105979

http://www.npr.org/2014/08/26/343484238/a-map-to-the-roots-of-fergusons-civic-unrest

8/26/14

The Attack Upon The Military Poor, the Middle Class and the Poor

First let's look at the Military on Food Stamps

http://www.truth-out.org/news/item/25807-about-620000-military-families-rely-on-food-pantries-to-meet-basic-needs

8/27/14

**The Larger Meaning of Ferguson--It Is Not Just About Race**

Now stepping back and looking all of this it is difficult not to ask the question "is all of this a deliberate, coordinated effort;" is it a perfect confluence of pre-existing racialized attitudes, in the US (now seen to be an example of prevalent racialized societies in most of the West;) allied with financial crunch attitudes where tribes start to look out only for their own when times get rough; where large sums of money are being spent to create and maintain divisions in society along racial, gender, economic and social lines to exploit and intensify hatreds and conflict.

Strife, conflicts and hatreds pay; and they exist because some in society benefit enormously from them, and in existing, others are designated to be crushed losers. Behind all the angst of these divisions hide the real powers that are pulling the strings, making money and never challenged.

The Banks fed off poverty as well.

http://rt.com/op-edge/182896-mortgage-scams-unpunished-ferguson-angry/

See also my "The History of Human Societies" to see these patterns at work across thousands of years of human history.

http://www.authorsden.com/visit/viewshortstory.asp?id=60893&authorid=121255

And:

http://www.authorsden.com/visit/viewshortstory.asp?id=61029&authorid=121255

Nothing scares powerful elites, bent on maintaining their power, more than seeing races and social groups begin to unite, rather than fight against each other.

These elites love divisions, deliberately sow discord, and note as well, that many in US society, for example, also depend upon these divisions for their daily livelihood, are emotionally enmeshed in families, groups, races which severely punish those who step outside the prevailing ethos, racial attitudes and the like, pushing the idea that divisions and hatreds are all part of some natural order of things (i.e., the poor will always be poor and with us; i.e., in life there are winners and losers;) all this designed to encourage acquiescence in the status quo.
.
Maintaining and enforcing this "culture of acceptance" of the unacceptable is parroted and reflected in the media, in the family, in subcultures, in the schools, in politics, at work, virtually everywhere. Superiors and inferiors are natural so goes the propaganda. The message is "count yourself lucky that you are not a target like the blacks. Look the other way."

See:
How personal values are superseded by those parroted propaganda messages in the media. A worldwide study.

http://www.sciencedaily.com/releases/2014/02/140224081027.htm

This is how attitudes become inculcated in a society and more or less become part of each of various sub-cultures and is maintained by a combination of social controls across an entire society where punishments and reinforcements are enmeshed in the very fabric of the culture; of people's lives. Done successfully, individuals fail to even question their circumstances or the prevalent order of things altogether.

This is where we are now. Rebellion against the prevailing ethos is stamped out with tanks and guns. This has happened over and over in history and it is happening now in the United States which is by no means the first time it has happened It is part of American History.

Ah, but what to do?  It is hopeless? Why no, of course not. What the human mind and hands have built they can change.

I have a few modest suggestions about how change is possible at:

http://www.authorsden.com/visit/viewshortstory.asp?id=61366&authorid=121255

8/28/14

The Impact of Racism on Whites

Now we look at the impact of racism on whites noting most whites have no idea of the negative impacts that such institutionalized racism has upon them and theirs.

Most of the white tribe see themselves:

1. As superior to virtually every black they meet (studies show this time and time again) and even

ones they never meet. Brain studies show that people and human recognition areas of the brain fail to light up when whites look at photos of blacks. They light up normally when viewing photos of whites. Failure to light up basically means most whites don't see blacks as human beings, therefore lack empathy for them, and basically see them as animals.
For men an additional basic reaction was that of fear and threat.

"Neuroscience has shown that people can identify another person's apparent race, gender, and age in a matter of milliseconds. In this blink of an eye, a complex network of stereotypes, emotional prejudices, and behavioral impulses activates. These knee-jerk reactions do not require conscious bigotry, though they are worsened by it."

More:

"Within a moment of seeing the photograph of an apparently homeless man, for instance, people's brains set off a sequence of reactions characteristic of disgust and avoidance. The activated areas included the insula, which is reliably associated with feelings of disgust toward objects such as garbage and human waste. Notably, the homeless people's photographs failed to stimulate areas of the brain that usually activate whenever people think about other people, or themselves. Toward the homeless (and drug addicts), these areas simply failed to light up, as if people had stumbled on a pile of trash."

From:

http://greatergood.berkeley.edu/article/item/look_twice

Now the depth of this unconscious racism despite what people say has some astounding aspects. Namely:

1. Both blacks and whites are racist to an uncomfortable degree and is in place by age three. Blacks have both varieties: self-racism and racist attitudes toward whites mixed in with other aspects including, feelings of inferiority, fear, anger and resentment and feelings of superiority towards whites as well.

2. That all this is learned and culturally inculcated by age three in institutions ranging from the media, (see above on media) from schools, from religion, (Jesus was Jewish and most certainly dark-skinned but media have transformed him into a white male) to work where inferior roles are usually assigned to blacks and dark-skinned individuals or other-color skinned people. It is like a color caste system.

3. History, for example, is blurred over and untruths are presented as fact. For example, most Americans don't know that World War II was waged by Hitler to rid the world of Jews and blacks (whom he thought were inferior and though they controlled America inferior as they were America could be easily defeated in war.) It was a war to enthrone the "Aryan Race" for a thousand years. So racism matters and millions of lives were lost and are lost today because such racism persists; ominously more that Hitler himself is that millions of Germans went along with this rant.

It is in all of us and this book will look at not only the details of its existence but also how it is created and maintained each generation. It is not inevitable, it is enforced. We will concentrate on the latter aspect in this book to some extent.

But for now we want to see the huge negative toil racism takes on our white brothers and sisters.

The first is that a racist system produces severe psychological, economic and often fatal results for whites.

Let's see how the psychological aspects work first.

The white psyche is haunted by fear, by visions of violence and threat. Seeing blacks, indeed any "other" as dangerous and a threat is common within the racist-inculcated culture.

Just look at American foreign policy. We have been in in Vietnam, in Iraq, in Afghanistan, in South America, all over the world, seeking out 'threats." Terrorists are everywhere and we kill them in villages and hamlets all over the planet and then wonder where terrorists come from, as populations strike back.

And creating more and more terrorists in this fashion is entirely functional for elites using terrorism as an excuse to maintain and extend their own power, profits for their arms dealers, power for the politicians, and jobs for their tribe.

These dynamics make our kids, indeed entire generations, clinical psychopaths, producing generations after generations, entirely void of any empathy for the suffering of others.

We kill in our media, in our video games, love to hunt and kill animals, hunt and kill in our cities, kill and sacrifice in our religion myths, love blood, and our unconscious is plagued by vision of vampires sucking our blood (a true metaphor that) and learn all the cultural skills of not seeing clearly any of this; avoidance of real facts in life are learned early.

In essence, we have a culture which enculturates generation after generation of American kids into how to become little psychopaths and rewards the most successful with leadership and positions of power.

See:

http://www.authorsden.com/visit/viewshortstory.asp?id=59847&authorid=121255

Actually, during most of my education exemplars such as generals and great civilizations were ones which subdued neighbors and murdered millions and created a unified state, through plunder and mayhem.

Why should I respect this? Only elites bent on the same and similar goals put this up and exposing me to it will make it seem reasonable and only pursuing 'greatness" dare I say "exceptionalism."  I am being conditioned to accept their goals as I grow up.

As one of my white friends said: "Actually I don't think about race and all this stuff at all." I said "Precisely Bill." We laughed.

As our first concrete example let's see what our media tells us about Unconscious America and what our media obsessions tells us about ourselves.

Our movies, TV, print and digital are preoccupied with murder, mayhem, threat, prejudices, vampires, dystopias, selfies, dismemberments and the like. Our media, in effect, create and nurture a constant sense of threat where the correct response is to slaughter the source of the threat. Let's have a look at this idea and see if it makes any sense. Then we come back to continue our examination, of other institutions. http://www.authorsden.com/visit/viewshortstory.asp?id=60169&authorid=121255

8/29/14

We look at the angry white male.

We look at individual statistics, domestic violence, gun mania and sales, drugs. Well the list is a long one indeed. What we want to know is if these items are to be taken as effect, or cause?

First let's look at some initial statistics on the white male in America.

They are incredibly revealing,

Oh. Next time, I have to run out and save the world. Be right back.

Back now.

First: The Angry White Male

"And many have moved from their deindustrializing cities, foreclosed suburban tracts, and wasted farmlands to smaller rural areas because they seek the companionship of like-minded fellows, in relatively remote areas far from large numbers of nonwhites and Jews and where they can organize, train, and build protective fortresses. Many groups have established refuge in rural communities, where they can practice military tactics, stockpile food and weapons, hone their survivalist skills, and become self-sufficient in preparation for Armageddon, the final race war, or whatever cataclysm they envision. Think of it as the twenty-first-century version of postwar suburban "white flight"—but on steroids."

"They're certainly Christian, but not just any Christian—they're evangelical Protestant, Pentacostalist, and members of radical sects that preach racial purity as the Word of Jesus. (Catholicism is certainly stocked with conservatives on social issues, but white supremacists tap into such a long and ignoble tradition of anti-Catholicism that they tend to have their own right-wing organizations, mostly fighting against women's rights and gay rights.) Some belong to churches like the Christian Identity Church, which gained a foothold on the Far Right in the early 1980s. Christian Identity's focus on racism and anti-Semitism provides the theological underpinnings to the shift from a more "traditional agrarian protest" to paramilitarism. It is from the Christian Identity movement that the Far Right gets its theological claims that Adam is the ancestor of the Caucasian race, whereas non-whites are pre-Adamic "mud people," without souls, and Jews are the children of Satan. According to this doctrine, Jesus was not Jewish and not from the Middle East; actually, he was northern European, his Second Coming is close at hand, and followers can hasten the apocalypse. It is the birthright of Anglo-Saxons to establish God's kingdom on earth; America's and

Britain's "birthright is to be the wealthiest, most powerful nations on earth . . . able, by divine right, to dominate and colonize the world."
Sorry to quote so much but this is a landmark article:

"Many of the younger guys are veterans of the first Gulf War, a war that they came to believe was fought for no moral principles at all, but simply to make America's oil supply safer and to protect Israel from possible Arab attack. They feel they've been used, pawns in a larger political game, serving their country honorably only to be spit out and stepped on when they returned home to slashed veteran benefits, bureaucratic indifference to post-traumatic stress disorder, and general social contempt for having fought in the war in the first place. They believed they were entitled to be hailed as heroes, as had earlier generations of American veterans, not to be scorned as outcasts. Now a guy like Bo Gritz symbolizes "true" warrior-style masculinity, and reclaiming their manhood is the reward for signing up with the Far Right."

"So, who are they really, these hundred thousand white supremacists? They're every white guy who believed that this land was his land, was made for you and me. They're every down-on-his-luck guy who just wanted to live a decent life but got stepped on, every character in a Bruce Springsteen or Merle Haggard song, every cop, soldier, auto mechanic, steelworker, and construction worker in America's small towns who can't make ends meet and wonders why everyone else is getting a break except him. But instead of becoming Tom Joad, a left-leaning populist, they take a hard right turn, ultimately supporting the very people who have dispossessed them."

From:

8/30/14

What do we make of the AWM grievances? Some seem patently absurd and I will look those in due turn. But first let's look at the ones which seem justified.

1 The AWM, his father and his father's father have been exploited, disinherited, and used. The family farm has been taxed such that they were broken up and gradually sold off piece by piece to agribusiness which came in with huge tax breaks, which meant higher taxes for other small land owners. They were zoned out with suburban creep, with federal water practices, with even the EPA and by NAFTA resulting in virtually pennies on the dollar for their crops. Massive debt ensued for these small farmers and their suppliers.
2. Without education, they had to leave their small towns, or starve, couldn't marry, and some went to the Gulf and took a lot of that bitterness with them. Compromised in their base beliefs they bought into the idea of bringing democracy to the hoards. But once there many realized that the war was indeed a sham and came home not to small town parades but

some scorn, little money, no medical care, and having to get food from the local food pantry to survive, Children they had never seen, wives divorced them and family life crumbled and they were forced to declare themselves PSDT in order to get disability money; this a major humiliation for these proud young men.

They drift into local bars, do domestic violence, drink, drugs, meth labs, sell grass, a lot of things to make ends meet.

On television they don't see themselves celebrated, rather they are demonized. It is the cops who get a lot of TV air and many, many of them become cops, become cops in Ferguson and in many of the small towns in America where they get the same gear they used in America's wars overseas.

'Now we see some of them on television.

More later.

9-1-14 Ferguson:

"The St. Louis suburb, where unarmed black teen Michael Brown was shot dead August 9 by white police officer Darren Wilson, has just over 21,000 residents and had more than 40,000 arrest warrants as of June 2013, according to ArchCity Defenders, a local advocacy group."

From:

http://www.aol.com/article/2014/08/25/outstanding-

See also:

 So we see here angry blacks and angry whites confronting each other and either side does not understand how that is happening and who is benefiting from this circumstance.

9/2/14

Now where do we go to from here? What do we make of the AWM in this looking to the future? The grievances above seem valid although the reaction to these grievances are extreme and often have murderous intent.

The interesting question here is why the legitimate anger has resolved itself upon blacks, Jews and the government in such irrational ways, blind anger; lashing out at minorities, and more feeling themselves to be victims in society.

It is easy to see how the divide and rule tactics of political, economic, media and cultural elites have had these folks focus that anger on the Jews, blacks, the government, Indians, Catholics, by a constant propaganda flow which identifies these groups as "threats." Notice how the appeal, in this frame, is to appeal to views of the world the AWM has been trained to see as "other" almost from birth. It is an easy task to focus it on what he/she has seen on TV for years, in video games, in movies, in print, in family attitudes toward those "others" such as blacks. Most of these guys know few blacks, Indians, or Jews.

Racism we see, therefore, creates psychological distortions among these folks, irrational views, and, ominously, they are armed, angry young men.

These pressures are well illustrated in the following article which contains the cultural myth about blacks and crime and the true facts about white on white crime.

"Yet the disturbing truth, according to the FBI's most recent homicide statistics, is that the United States is in the wake of an epidemic of white-on-white crime. Back in 2011, the most recent year for which data is available, a staggering 83 percent of white murder victims was killed by fellow Caucasians."

From:

http://www.vox.com/2014/8/21/6053811/white-on-white-murder

More on actual crime rates in the United States:

http://www.theroot.com/articles/culture/2012/04/white onwhite_crime_it_goes_against_the_false_media_nar rative.html

"The truth? As the largest racial group, whites commit the majority of crimes in America. In particular, whites are responsible for the vast majority of violent crimes. With respect to aggravated assault, whites led blacks 2-1 in arrests; in forcible-rape cases, whites led all racial and ethnic groups by more than 2-1. And in larceny theft, whites led blacks, again, more than 2-1."

Yet, as I keep iterating, whites are propagandized daily in the media to see blacks as a violent threat when clearly this is not the case.

FBI Crime Statistics

http://www.fbi.gov/about-us/cjis/ucr/crime-in-the-u.s/2011/crime-in-the-u.s.-2011/tables/table-43

So what are to the solutions to this volatile situation?

9/2/14

For those who want to jump ahead to possible larger political and social issues and solutions take a look at these videos which show not only how change occurs but also how counter-changes occur.

http://www.youtube.com/watch?feature=player_detailpage&v=puusxNAkoe4


http://www.youtube.com/watch?feature=player_detailpage&v=jWaR5JRG0lo

How do all these ideas hang together and what is my point? We are back tomorrow to put them all together.

9/3/14

Now, you ask, how do these ideas thus far cohere? Ferguson, political history, conservatism, liberalism etc. Well, they do, and we take a look.

I assume that you dear reader have read the following already-blogs which deal with race, discrimination, the history of human societies and specific tactics elites have used historically, to control the populations under their control.

(Note control strategies used by elites against their populations are identical to those recommended in the book "The Art of War:" this is the bible of big business. See "The Art of War" by Sun Tzu at:

http://en.wikipedia.org/wiki/The_Art_of_War

The previous blogs are listed below.

http://www.authorsden.com/visit/viewshortstory.asp?id=61331&authorid=121255

http://www.authorsden.com/visit/viewshortstory.asp?id=60893&authorid=121255

http://www.authorsden.com/visit/viewshortstory.asp?id=61029&authorid=121255

What we propose now is to examine what goes for right, left, center and far right in politics today and we come to the conclusion that there is mass confusion in the political realm in the West.

Here are a few points which are seldom discussed in today's political discourse.

1. The Founding Generation of the United States was part of the enlightenment and was clearly anti-

government having experienced centuries of kingly, religious, slavery and military domination. They rose against over-weaning powerful government championing reason, individual rights and limited and small government. They created and were the authors of liberalism.

Today these ideas are championed by what is regarded as the far-right wing in politics, adding into the mix portions of racisms, states, extreme nationalism along the way and a mania for guns to resist authority.

Now we want to ponder the question of how did this political reversal  and confusion occur because we see former liberals now championing big government, collective rights, community rule and structure, socialism and various stripes of Marxism, decentralization, worker rights and an incrementalism which argues for inclusion in the current political structure not its total destruction, an anti-nationalism, and a modification ethic; to be contrasted with the far-right vision of secession, ala the South in the pre-civil war era.

How did this flip flop occur? We will take a look.

The connection is that Ferguson can be seen to exemplify blacks wanting big government, active government to intervene and help protect their civil and other rights, while many in the police, are operating from a military tradition operating from an ethos of serving the state in protecting the state and society from would be rebels and revolutionaries and enemies of the state.
Now you can see the confusion and contradictions

here.

How to sort all this out, but more importantly what is to be the way and means toward clarity not only in terms of ideas and but down on the ground as well.

Our goal is no mere academic one because once these dynamics are understood and sorted out; we can identify solution sets that do not pit society and social groups against one another, but solutions that work for all. I know, ambitious. But the goal is not to construct utopia, but to avoid dystopia.

Hint: a key driver will be the altered and changed roles of those who control what used to be called the political economy. No, hang on there, it will not be boring. I promise.

9/4/14

The success of the liberal movement in the 18th and 19th centuries was based on several approaches and factors which enabled the liberal movement to effect broad changes in societies across Europe. Monarchy after monarchy fell, peasants, and serfs freed, revolutions occurred...

1. They attacked the monarchies and aristocrats from several vantage points, economic, social, cultural and political, simultaneously.

   a. They organized the burgeoning middle and lower classes holding house hold meetings, took advantage of mass printing for the first time, attacking specific problems, like slavery, working conditions, hierarchy and offering specific solutions, rather than putting out mass utopia solutions as goals. They sought critical solutions which taken together transformed the whole of society in a period of just twenty to thirty years in some cases.

b. They advanced moral rather that political, or economic arguments, understanding that arguments based upon reason in fact have to be presented with an undertone of emotional outrage using the fulcrum ideas of fairness, equality and justice, and above all the idea of freedom from state power. Dr; Martin Luther King, Gandhi effected change in exactly this way.

c. They understood that a plurality of strong institutions in society, from the family, to small business, small farmers, communication conduits, a readiness to act were the main ways in which to undermine state power. The would be dictatorial state seek to have nothing between itself and the individual-rending the individual powerless against its massive state institutions.

Social, economic, cultural institutions were created and became the main bulwarks against state power. Even militia power was to be counter-balanced against state means of violence, such that they were effective deterrents against the state actually using its military might, if only because there were many, many citizens scattered across the country.

They understood that weak social, political and economic institutions is the goal of over-weaning power, thus they supported all these institutions as inoculations against state power. They won most of their goals and gave us modern societies.

But it was not to last.

Next we want to look at why they failed to stand up to counter-change forces which sought to re-assert state power.

Now even in the liberal victory against the monarchies, there were several weaknesses which we explore next time, weaknesses which exposed them to a counter-revolution which gives us the current worldwide power configuration in the west.

Summary:

Weak institutions are the goal of would-be power mongers in society because it eliminates internal sources of resistance. The goal is to purposely weakened any and all such institutions, keep the citizens poor, dependent, fearful and willing to turn on their neighbors and willing to exchange their rights and freedoms for "security."

By way of circumlocution: Ferguson and black and white communities over the years have been deliberately weakened in order to prevent them from rebelling against authority, local state or national. They have been weakened by infusion of drugs, by attacking the family, by sowing internal divisions in communities between blacks and whites, between the sexes, gay and straight, police and blacks, over teachers and schools, and violence if necessary if none of that works. These are classic maneuvers used by elites for centuries.

Time to get smart about it.

All this is not random; this is what is taught elites in those ivy league colleges and boarding schools.

9/4/14

Is local government an answer and counter weight to state and national power. How is that working out?

Small Towns: Why Some Hate Them and Leave and Why Some Stay.

For an insightful look at the dictatorial tendencies of local authority and typical small town politics see:

https://www.youtube.com/watch?feature=player_detail page&v=2j0p1Zs78bU

Next time we detail how liberals lost their hard won victories and, however, how they can get their mojo back.

Hint:
The focus on government power changes totally if counter forces capture government power and imagery.

9/5/14

Here is what went wrong with liberal adherents:

1. Their victory complete, liberals simply did not remain vigilant against the counter revolution state power-mongers mounted after the 1890's in the United States. The era of the robber barons and the

rise of modern industrial capitalism caught the liberal thinkers by surprise and they had no ready answer to the re-concentration of wealth and power in the hands of these new capitalist elites.

2. Their power base lay in small groups, in the so-called petite bourgeoisie,

in the guild system and in labor groups; in small family merchant and farm sectors were also eroded. Their think tanks moved from face to face discussions, from the solon to idea generation being taken over by the university set.

3. They failed to see that economic power increasingly captured political power and limited government became increasingly powerful government.

4. They failed to understand the 1913 creation of the Federal Reserve Bank controlled by bankers was as a direct threat to liberal ideas, politics and governmental structure.

5. They failed to see how this new statism, masking itself as patriotism, would and did lead to World War 1 where that war would destroy the basis of prosperity in most countries and that war against the "Hun" would allow resurgent elites to introduce a racism which would combine with nationalism and fascism and ultimately lead to Hitler and World War 11.

In sum, the resurgence of over-weaning state power was back now with an admixture of the above elements and you get the far-right of today. One strain ant-government but having also absorbed fascist,

Nazi, nationalist, and aggressive tendencies which themselves gave the world imperialism as a book-end to these nationalist tendencies.

6. Add to these in later decades, Reaganism, Thatcherism, Globalism in the 20th and 21st centuries and the liberal plight came into sharp focus. Insult to injury classical liberals bemoaned this as "neo-liberalism" besmirching their own past.

Prosperity which was  so key to the rise of liberalism facilitated the rise of the middle class 190 years ago is and had been replaced by wars which destroyed value, and created boom and bust cycles, which have and currently do destabilize the poor and middle class, appropriating their wealth in these recurrent boom and bust cycles. These groups and other institutions in society have been weakened or co-opted such that they do not and have been made to believe they cannot challenge these new wall street led elites. This weakening of liberal institutions, mind you, is and was no accident.

Ok, now that I have depressed you; next time we look at solutions

12/2/14

All of the coverage of Ferguson after the verdict around the world.

1/22/14 Six Videos and articles on Coverage of the upcoming grand jury decision in Ferguson

10/26/14 New Autopsy Results on the other police shooting contradicts police claims

10/23/14 Brown autopsy results revealed. Clashes start up again

10/12/14 "Ferguson October" National Coverage Updates: On Ferguson: The Latest

9/13/14 How Organizing Can Be Used-Not Just For Poor Communities.

9/11/14 Community Organizing: Chapter Four

9/10/14 Community Organizing: Chapter Three

9/9/14 Ferguson City Council Vows Reforms

9/9/14 Chapter Two of the Organizer's Handbook

9/8/14 The Sure-Fire, Inexpensive Plan For Community Change. Today: First Steps

9/8/14 How to effect change in communities from the bottom up.

9/6/14

What do liberals have to do?

1. Eschew strictly moral political arguments and understand that the poor have to eat. The separation of the middle classes from the poor weakened the middle class which in turn made a pact with the new economic elites in a new "Jobism" ethic which essentially was and is co-opting of the middle class.

The middle class was afraid to maintain its poor relations connections for fear that this would not be acceptable to the new corporate bosses. The poor were abandoned by the middle class here in the US. But this was not some much the case in Europe. The two classes were diluted in a proportional representation system but maintained contact working together in a system to promote prosperity to raise all ships. (However, immigration in Europe has created a similar scenario where the middle class have not supported the immigrants leading to an resurgence of the right wing in many countries.)

In the US, rampant cowboy privatization has prevailed.

Solution? The middle class has to re-establish its coalition with the poor and together move forward.. The middle classes usually provide the leadership and the poor provide the streets and the down on the ground organizations.

2. The liberals have to take the battle to the local level and not sit in leather chairs moralizing. Unfortunately, as we see above in earmarking education as key to "Jobism" the middle class left the small towns for college and privatization; if they returned they made sure they separated themselves from the poor by settling on the right side of the tracks.
Summary point: Engage the poor, organize.

3. In a confused political situation such as we have in the US today a good example of implementing social change is to look at how the gay community reversed American opinion in less than twenty years and overcame even certain legal barriers. That campaign is a good example of how to achieve social change.

Note it had the very same multi-faceted character as the liberal campaign a century and a half earlier, utilizing many strategies simultaneously. It worked then and is working for the gay community currently.

4. Become political. Occupy refused to and did not post demands or a strategy other than trying to build a street community which was not enough. Make demands, get political and stay in the streets as long as it takes. That tactic brought down slavery.

5. Liberals and now libertarians, have to understand that anti-government attitudes play into the hands of the opposition in as much as conservatives control politics but they in turn are controlled by Wall Street and are ineffective. So what to do?
Simple, go to the root of the problem: don't allow Wall Street to control you by giving them your money every month coming from your paychecks. 100k people withdrawing their money from wall street banks, setting up local and state banks, having unions and liberal billionaires do the same will bring Wall Street down or to the negotiating table quickly.

Who Controls World Finances?

http://www.youtube.com/watch?feature=player_detail page&v=cOZ2I6UNY34

6. Stop complaining about the culture, about institutions, about poverty, learn to pool resources, take advantage of modern social media and understand that liberals have to provide, in as much as possible, alternatives services and jobs for their supporters. The right wing has done that with Koch Brothers money.

Their secret is simple; they provide jobs, and an alternative community to join. Liberals have to do that as well, and the structure is already there to do it. Bottom up social media is an obvious example, citizen reporting such as I do is another. But liberals themselves are locked into "Jobism" and wall street so much they don't feel they can risk switching horses. Have to make it worth it for them.

7. Divide and Rule: Look at the Conservative repressive play book and use the same tactics against them. They fund music which advocates generation divisions, TV which reinforces that division between young and old, family strife and arguments, literature which reinforces the notion of strife and division. it is everywhere and that is no accident. We must begin to unify not continue division because unified social, political and economic groups is the only remedy against these divide and rule tactics.

In politics the failure to exploit the enormous contradiction where poor whites support the very same parties and class which exploits them is an obvious point. I believe the angry white male and poor whites, churches and social media are obvious places to begin to post unity messages, coming together messages and show people how it would benefit them to switch horses and abandon race, sex, sexual orientations as ways to make political allegiances, social, and economic decisions.

Summary: Look at the play book outlined in this book identifying how elites have dominated populations over centuries and copy them (except for the violent tactics.) We have examples from the liberal campaigns all the way to Dr. Martin Luther King.

Ferguson is an example where liberals failed to show up or speak out, not even for free speech, fairness, and the like-the traditional stances real liberals have always stood for. No, they stood by silent, an enforced silence, fearful, job and endorsement obsessed, and not really comfortable with the images of poor people they were seeing on their TV screens. Their parents had spent their childhood basically saying "poverty is the worst thing in the world, become a wage slave."

Well poverty is not the worst thing in the world if it becomes the spring board for organizing, and that is what the people of Ferguson did, and that effort rang around the world.

Now is the time for persistence, not tisk-tisking and teeth sucking.

For background on the above points see:

"The Middle Class and The Poor:

http://www.authorsden.com/visit/viewshortstory.asp?id=54046&authorid=121255

Self-Sufficiency

http://www.authorsden.com/visit/viewshortstory.asp?id=53669&authorid=121255

http://www.authorsden.com/visit/viewshortstory.asp?id=53990&authorid=121255

9/7/14:

Note the contradictions in that conservatives rail against big  government while being its primary beneficiaries. How even the Founding Generation did not have the common man in mind revealing themselves as not really liberals, prompting true liberals in America to demand a bill of rights be attached to the constitution.

Moral of the story: no one is to be trusted with absolute or great power, least of all conservatives. They have a bad track record going back thousands of years.

Beware of power-mongers using the power of the state for their freedom against the freedoms of others.

So what is the best political configuration with a world history which clearly shows that politics has mostly been about using power to decide "who gets what, when, where and how" and distributing power, money and wealth to friends and allies; and about maintaining that power and expanding it internally as well as externally-using violence if necessary?

9/9/14

Update On Ferguson. Seems we were right on the traffic tax on poor communities.

"A 2013 report by the Missouri attorney general's office found that Ferguson police stopped and arrested black drivers nearly twice as often as white motorists, but were also less likely to find contraband among the black drivers.

In Ferguson, court fines and fees accounted for $2.6 million in the last fiscal year, or nearly one-fifth of the city budget. That's nearly twice as much as the city collected just two years earlier.

Of the 90 municipal governments in St. Louis County, 22 depend on such fines for at least one-fifth of their revenue. An Associated Press analysis shows that 38 towns or villages depend on municipal fines from minor traffic violations for at least one-tenth of their annual revenue. Three cities with 1,000 or fewer people rely on municipal fines for the majority of their yearly income."

More:

"The report by the nonprofit ArchCity Defenders found dozens of cases where children and members of the public were improperly banned from attending open court session. In Ferguson, defendants described a system so overwhelmed by crowds that bailiffs would lock the door five minutes after the scheduled start time — and then issue failure to appear warrants for those who arrived late and were locked out. In Bel-Ridge, multiple defendants were in court to contest citations for not registering with the city garbage collection service."

http://abcnews.go.com/US/wireStory/ferguson-city-council-plans-review-board-25368583


http://www.washingtonpost.com/news/post-nation/wp/2014/09/09/what-to-expect-at-fergusons-first-council-meeting-since-the-michael-brown-shooting/

http://www.npr.org/player/v2/mediaPlayer.html?action=1&t=1&islist=false&id=343143937&m=343203899

Bringing the story of Ferguson Down and Personal

http://www.washingtonpost.com/news/the-watch/wp/2014/09/03/how-st-louis-county-missouri-profits-from-poverty/

http://www.nytimes.com/2014/09/13/us/mistrust-lingers-as-ferguson-takes-new-tack-on-fines.html?_r=0

Indictment: Not Likely?

http://www.washingtonpost.com/opinions/dana-milbank-ferguson-tragedy-becoming-a-farce/2014/09/12/e52226ca-3a82-11e4-9c9f-ebb47272e40e_story.html

9/8/14

Today we move to the blueprint of how to organize change in poor and other communities from the bottom up.

First we want to identify the problems and then identify solutions which do work and have worked to remedy these problems.

Let's take Ferguson as our starting off point?

What are the problems: They are:

1. A justice system out of control
2. Grinding poverty
3. Hopelessness
4. Lack of those skills for self-improvement and advancement
5. The indifference of the larger white communities
6. Housing
7. Jobs
8. Education
9. Political Skills
10. Social and Social Media Skills
11. Huge incarceration rates
12. Rampant Racism

Note this list is the same list for any group, for Latinos, for American Indians women, etc,.
It was and is the same list for any immigrant group in any country. We will spell historically how groups have managed to move up from powerlessness to empowerment. hopelessness to hope, from apathy to mounting successful campaigns for change. I further note that most of these must be done simultaneously if possible because succeeding with one strategy helps implement the others.

9/8/14

The Sure-Fire, Inexpensive Social Change Kit- The Organizers Handbook

First, you want to get your posse together, that is three or four like-minded individuals whom you think will be willing to volunteer to get you through the first stage of organizing. It might be a local teacher, a retired person, older kids, anyone who is fired up about the need for change.

Hold meetings in a home, if not try the library, or the local church, where you will use the meetings to lay out the community action plan. (Always good to have "action" in a title for each plan and for the group as a whole. "Action" denotes more than talk.

At the first meeting, aside from introductions, you want get a sense of the skills of those in the room and their sense of other volunteers they might identify and their skills. You want to get a least six more volunteers to join your group and tell them what your plan is for them once they assemble. That plan will include:

1. Identification of resources needed.

Tell them the group will need one or more computers: a printer, access to Wi-Fi, a person with a car who can help with transportation needs and used cell phones. They will use the equipment to have the volunteers accumulate the following email lists and addresses:

a. First go to Melissa Data.com and download the following mailing lists: every non-profit in your zip code, what their budgets are, how many staff they have on board, their political giving patterns, and more. All of this free at Melissa Data.

For more detail go on the net to look up the non-profits in your area, their 990 forms, a form every non-profit must submit each year. This will give you more detail on the non-profits in your zip code and in zip codes near you.

b. Do the same for churches in your area; franchise restaurants, zoning commissioners, local, state and national representatives, local school boards, get names if you can, local merchants and small store owners, get the census tract data for your town or area, police data, local media, editors and reporters, and rates for a nearby Kinkos or a way to get stuff printed. The library sometimes can help or a local merchant who you can get to donate printing rather than money.

This is the first stage of your action plan now on paper, it is your way to mobilize support quickly and easily for issues you and your action group will want to put forth seeking support. That is why we need six volunteers, to make those calls looking for support to get the data in this first stage.

You want them to start to make the first calls also to recruit more volunteers and to acquaint the email list with news about your group starting up. Ask them for at least three things: 1. Please join us, if not donate stuff to us, if not identify three people they recommend you call, and if not threaten to call them back later.

Now with twelve volunteers, it is time to evaluate how things are going, survey the materials at hand, and the larger group will develop next step strategies. What is that?

9/9/14

Second: With 12 volunteers or less you can start a JTST program. This would be jobs, training, service and tutoring program.

Now you want to identify volunteers who will take on the following tasks.

1. Print up flyers, compose emails to announce your new action plan for the community.

2. Assign volunteers to recruit more volunteers in the following ways and from the following sources.

Visit local churches seeking support for your program called "Help One At A Time" asking that the church help you recruit one individual at a time to be screened and trained to be tutored and made eligible for your job training program JTST. Church members would take on that task after school and the goals would be to get the kids after school jobs and internships in the community..

After the churches do the screening and referrals you approach local non-profits: sit with their board of directors and officers and explain you need their help with after school tutoring and training where non-profits would create an after school training program where the trainers would be their own non-profit staffs to be paid five dollars an hour to train kids in skills ranging from use of business software to office decorum using the non-profits own computers and equipment. The kids would repay the training given them with their own free labor. The non-profits could eventually get this program funded with grants and/or donations from the community.

This idea of free labor for training (we did this in Berkeley and San Francisco and it works) can be expanded to local merchants and shop owners improving community relations immensely. Small shop owners, gas stations, doctors, dentists, etc., all can use the extra help from your carefully screened kids and sign a contract that if the kid works out he/she will eventually get a stipend after 3 to six months. Valuable skills can be learned and taught in a small business. Once kids get some training, they can be sent to larger firms as interns, temp agencies and get better paying jobs with references,
No news travels faster in poor neighborhoods than news about jobs.

Of course you will need volunteer drivers to help out as well.

Those on probation, on in the Criminal Justice System already need special programs which we outline at a later date.

Future components of community organizing will include:

1. A media campaign with the group developing its own videos, on-line newspapers and its own on-line radio show (all free on the internet)
2. Give-Back Programs where the kids once trained train other kids and in those very same non-profits helping the non-profit and the kids imparting skills they have learned to younger kids

We will explore in the future, setting up food banks, federal and state programs available, STEM programming (35 dollar computers are available now) and we can use used cell phones as well for access to the internet.

We will explore small businesses staffed by young people, everything from clean-up, house painting, car washes, bake sales, thrift sales, a lot.

We will explore shopping coops to save money.

There will be petition and voter drives, car donation drives, family bank trainings, homeless programs, zoning changes to clean up the neighborhood, allow in-laws apartments to house the young who cannot afford a huge home or even an apartment; teach people how to step up and use social media, especially a twitter account and a face book account, free music sessions, and getting involved in politics to protect the community.

Getting enough people involved will create a critical mass at some point and group pride and sense of effectiveness will grow. One simple rule I like to establish: celebrate small successes, be patient and look for opportunities to strengthen the community.

All this can grow beyond the community into neighboring communities as communities come together to support one another discovering they have issues in common.

This is not only possible, this is how America became America. It can be done again.

**9/10/14**

**Chapter Three of the Organizers Handbook**

Now at this third phase we want to focus on:

Introducing ourselves to the community, telling people about the goals of the organization and getting input and more support from the community members who want to help.

First the media campaign:
You will want to:
a. Go to city hall meetings there to make introductions but to meet other individuals and groups already involved in the community. Have business cards and flyers if you can and a signup sheet to get names addresses and emails for further contact. Do this at every event you go to, that way you build up your own mailing list.

If you are clever go to the meeting early, have people sign your sheets and move on another meeting. That way you can do several a night.

You will want to get your own free radio show going. Try BlogTalkRadio. It is free and relatively easy to navigate, but notice when you get one and your youngsters trained do a show, it helps in approaching non-profits and churches because you can offer them support in setting up their own radio shows. You are building support in this matter. Again, offer to train their young people in how to do it, and the Board of Directors as well, as a means to publicize their meetings and events. You also do music on these shows and how-to segments for your adults and kids.

Get local music groups together and use the free media to publicize their music. You can see the possibilities.

Ditto on getting your own newspaper going. Try Paper.li.com. It is free. You can use it to give, in one spot, all of your announcements, and with a weekly, people can catch up on activities they missed.

Now secondly in this phase, or sooner if necessary, you can identify volunteers to help with jobs, with food and transportation. These are key and you can get support for your group if you offer free labor from the younger kids and older ones as well.

Jobs come from training the kids and having the older kids train the younger ones, getting that five dollars non-profits were paying their staff. Now you can transition to the other steps outlined above and ultimately get people trained on common office software like Word, and Excel. From there on to temp agencies for jobs. Temps get hired permanently 40% of the time.

But you have to train your people to pass the temp office skills test. More on that later.

Food: A food pantry is essential. You can look at state programs, food banks, and also local and chain restaurants. They throw away a lot of food and you want to talk to them about donating food for free labor. This is a good exchange since kids bringing food home from free labor jobs for the family is esteem building for all concerned.

Next time we continue with Phase Three Jobs, Health, zoning, Politics, personal assistants, researchers, code, downtown equipment use, babysitting, finders clubs, teen businesses, and more.

9/11/14

Ok folks "The Ferguson Chronicles" will be a book in about two weeks. Let me suggest that I give you the chapter headings and information as guidance to those of you who want to continue working.

Thanks for all support and encouragement. Turns out anyone who wants to organize communities for virtually any purpose can use this handbook to get the job done.

Now for the headings:

You may now understand some of them and hopefully you will support the effort and donate to the cause by buying my book or PayPal me with a small donation to get the book publicized so others can also benefit from the information. PayPal your donation to my email address at lonnie.hicks@gmail.com

8-23-14
Website: www.lonniehicks.com

All Help Welcomed

Also I do telephone consulting if you need help getting started in your community. These ideas work in any community for any cause.

Now in phase three we concentrate on:

Jobs, Food, and Media and developing our volunteer cadres. This goes along with developing community ties by providing service to the community in the form of free labor, information and training.

Also you show the community how you can help with their individual and group goals and activities by sharing information, labor and ideas you have.

Ok. here we go.

You can reduce the need for money by doing direct bartering of services and by creating mini businesses. Here are a few ideas:

1. Develop a "Finder's Club" with your local church members. People need baby-sitting, houses painted, cars, food shopping and other services and information and can't pay middle class prices.

A telephone "Finders Club" phone number and your people put people in touch with those willing to provide those services and no or low prices. No cost is a bartering strategy for those with no money: "I baby sit your kids for two hours in exchange for you babysitting my kids for two hours."

The Finder's Club helps match people looking for that deal, working the phones in the church basement, in an extra room at the school. All you need is a phone and a list who is willing to participate and what services they are willing to swap.

You could call nearby chains and office buildings and propose an after work program for your kids where all those office spaces, empty after five pm could be used as spaces to train your kids on the latest office equipment. Your local temp agency could be tapped for volunteers to train those kids to pass the temp test on the latest office equipment.

(All these are actual programs I have created and ran for many years in the Bay Area.)

Have the Ferguson police department take in a few interns for training on all that equipment they are getting from the Federal Government. Training is training, community building is community building.

Now looking ahead think:

1. A legal defense fund, to get your people out of jail. Ask local firms for pro-bono defense support or to take one or two of your kids as interns in understanding what a lawyer does.

2.Get a door to door canvassing operation going informing people of your efforts and asking them to support your "Dollar--A-Week" Fund. Use the money for food, transportation and what not. If everyone Ferguson donated a dollar for themselves and donate in the name of others as well, you would have 21 thousand dollars a week to work with. Even if you don't get anywhere near that amount the PR you would have created would be invaluable.

3. Start a Family Bank, asking employers, neighbors to have their paychecks, and other income be deposited in the family bank rather than in the wall street banks, Chase, Wells, Citi etc. Call it an "Community Investment Club" to get around the laws wall street has created to squash small bank competition.

Have the churches do it, small merchants and well. This could be done entirely on line with no interest rate loans etc.
Help them do it.

If done enough, people could get no interest and low cost emergency, house, car loans and not have to pay high usurious interest rates from the predatory banks. Do it all on the internet or from the church basement.
That money could then be loaned out  for health emergency loans and/ or to add on a room so grandma didn't have to go the nursing home; or to square all those ridiculous fines small towns levy.

In fact you want a lawsuit to get back all those illegal fines extracted from the poor people. Find some smart lawyer, start the suit, since Ferguson has already admitted in public many were illegal. You want your money back not just an apology. A lawyer would take the case with minimum or no fee, since even if Ferguson is broke, legally the state could also be held liable for letting it happen.

See: "The Family Bank" below for details on the Family Bank.

http://www.authorsden.com/visit/viewshortstory.asp?id=53669&authorid=121255

How non-profits can use social media to raise money

http://www.authorsden.com/visit/viewshortstory.asp?id=56608&authorid=121255

Sample of A radio show:

http://www.blogtalkradio.com/lonniehicks

9/12/14

To answer the question of whether these ideas are for poor communities only.

No, they are the pretty much used in everything from presidential campaigns (Obama used them, remember he was an organizer) the republicans used them with the variant of capturing local radio and media, and local neighbor groups and door to door canvassing, of course has a long and distinguished history. The American revolutionaries also used the18th century's variant on these ideas.

So they do have universal application.

I have varied them here, adopting for the Ferguson situation, but they could be used for anything from getting more YMCA members to recruiting for book clubs.

Next time, I will look at how to mount regional and national campaigns,
after finishing up chapter headings for the new book.

9/29/14

"Price-gouging for government files is one way that local, state and federal agencies have responded to requests for potentially embarrassing information they may not want released. Open records laws are designed to give the public access to government records at little or no cost, and have historically exposed waste, wrongdoing and corruption."

http://www.cbsnews.com/news/ferguson-fee-to-turn-over-brown-files-10-times-a-city-workers-salary/

http://nation.foxnews.com/2014/09/28/justice-department-tells-ferguson-police-stop-wearing-bracelets-supporting-darren-wilson

http://touch.latimes.com/#section/-1/article/p2p-81526830/

"Organizations like the website Buzz feed were told they'd have to pay unspecified thousands of dollars for emails and memos about Ferguson's traffic-citation policies and changes to local elections. The

Washington Post said Ferguson wanted no less than $200 for its requests."

Police shooting in Ferguson

http://www.cbsnews.com/news/police-officer-shot-in-ferguson-missouri/

http://abcnews.go.com/US/wireStory/grand-jury-2nd-case-ferguson-officer-25841384

http://www.nytimes.com/2014/09/29/us/police-officer-shot-in-ferguson.html?_r=0

10/12/14 "Ferguson October" with all of media coverage. At:

http://www.huffingtonpost.com/2014/10/11/ferguson-october-protesters-streets_n_5971106.html

10/23/14 Brown autopsy results revealed. Clashes

http://www.cnn.com/2014/10/22/justice/ferguson-michael-brown-autopsy/

http://touch.latimes.com/#section/-1/article/p2p-81753149/

10/26/14

Family autopsy report on other shooting in St. Louis contradicts police report on the shooting.

http://rt.com/usa/198908-autopsy-st-louis-myers/

11/22/14

News Coverage: Just before the decision

http://www.cnn.com/2014/11/21/us/ferguson-grand-jury-ruling/index.html?iid=article_sidebar

http://www.cnn.com/2014/11/22/us/ferguson-grand-jury-ruling/

http://www.cnn.com/2014/11/21/us/ferguson-grand-jury-ruling/index.html?iid=article_sidebar

http://www.cnn.com/2014/11/18/justice/ferguson-grand-jury-charges/index.html?iid=article_sidebar

http://www.washingtonpost.com/politics/ferguson-police-officer-darren-wilson-has-mastered-a-disappearing-act-since-shooting/2014/11/21/2a4fc4cc-71cf-11e4-893f-86bd390a3340_story.html?tid=pm_national_pop

NY Brooklyn Shooting

http://newyork.cbslocal.com/2014/11/21/nypd-investigating-fatal-police-involved-shooting-inside-brooklyn-housing-complex/

The Battle of the Autopsies

http://www.pbs.org/newshour/rundown/michael-browns-official-autopsy-report-actually-reveal/

11/25/14
All of the Ferguson Coverage as of the above date.

http://www.democracynow.org/

http://rt.com/usa/208703-ferguson-transcript-brown-wilson/

http://mobile.bloomberg.com/news/2014-11-24/ferguson-protests-widen-to-include-police-killings-elsewhere.html

http://www.theguardian.com/us-news/live/2014/nov/25/ferguson-protests-turn-violent-after-grand-jury-verdict-live-updates

http://www.theguardian.com/music/2014/nov/25/q-tip-macklemore-ferguson-protests-rihanna-pharrell-killer-mike-talib-kweli

http://www.cbsnews.com/news/ferguson-grand-jury-decision-sparks-protests-nationwide/

http://www.usatoday.com/news/

http://www.scribd.com/doc/248128351/Darren-Wilson-Testimony

http://ktla.com/2014/11/24/violent-protests-spread-far-beyond-ferguson/

http://www.denverpost.com/news/ci_27006383/protesters-denver-decry-grand-jury-decision-ferguson

http://www.sacbee.com/news/local/article4131379.html

http://www.chicagobusiness.com/article/20141124/NEWS04/141129890?template=mobilehttp://www.huffingtonpost.com/2014/11/24/ferguson-grand-jury_n_6214686.html

http://www.npr.org/blogs/itsallpolitics/2014/11/25/366527106/federal-ferguson-investigation-will-remain-independent-holder-insists

rt coverage

http://rt.com/usa/

More on using traffic fines and arrest in exploiting and preying upon the poor not only in Ferguson but across the country.

http://qz.com/257042/these-seven-charts-explain-how-ferguson-and-many-other-us-cities-wring-revenue-from-black-people-and-the-poor/

http://www.washingtonpost.com/news/the-watch/wp/2014/09/03/how-st-louis-county-missouri-profits-from-poverty/

http://www.huffingtonpost.com/2014/08/22/ferguson-black-america_n_5694364.html

12/2/14

40 Million Dollars in lawsuits

http://www.reuters.com/article/2014/08/28/us-usa-missouri-shooting-idUSKBN0GS2KD20140828

Social Media

http://www.usatoday.com/story/news/nation/2014/11/18/ferguson-black-arrest-rates/19043207/

http://t.co/9cV5ipmORv … Dec 03, 2014 🔗

- http://t.co/r8L7JZTp62 police killing in deadly #Garner choke hold case #nyc #Ferguson http://t.co/BcQqMi37y7 Dec 03, 2014 🔗

- Occupy Wall Street volunteers defend #Ferguson protesters in court — RT USA http://t.co/OewQLyjEln Dec 03, 2014 🔗

#KKK flyer promising "lethal force" in #Ferguson at: http://t.co/EMWZvJWjSE … Dec 03, 2014 🔗

#Ferguson: Murdered black man a key witness in the Brown killing & set on fire. Where is the investigation? http://t.co/mazDqlxlJ9 …

- #Police shootings cost cites millions: See: http://t.co/6LtF3xxDc2 Dec 03, 2014 🔗

- Here is the #Chicago #Police and #Torture #Genocide #UN action: at: #Ferguson https://t.co/Y91iDKZdLQ #NYC Wall street worried about possible #Elizabeth Warren run for the

Presidency. http://t.co/EOPqlLms8S Dec 20, 2014 🔗

- #CNN #askacop show bombs: heavy twitter backlash. #Ferguson #blacklivesmatter #berkeleyprotests http://t.co/GuKtNIbU2r Dec 20, 2014 🔗
- #Ferguson DA finally speaks: #blacklivesmatter #handsupwalkout #ericgarner #icantbreathe # protests http://t.co/Z5e2x74LyH Dec 20, 2014 🔗
- #FBI Mishandled evidence: may affect thousands of cases http://t.co/7nmpykANX5 Dec 20, 2014 🔗
- Missouri AG sues municipalities for preying on minorities & not sharing proceeds illegally with the state. Really. http://t.co/JvdcvsAk3Z Dec 20, 2014 🔗
- #nazispotter war criminals received social security payments for years? . http://t.co/eojpZ8PVnI Dec 20, 2014 🔗
- Yes please buy my books cheapest only 2$ each. Make my holidays. Dec 20, 2014 🔗
- Author? Yes see http://t.co/rSzulXDL8w. 16 books. See Amazon too. Click Amazon glyph on my Web site. See 2$ Pdf cheap books too at my site. $ Dec 20, 2014 🔗
- No I am one of the few twitter authors who really interact with my readers, and others on

twitter. I taught for years so it's natural to me. Dec 20, 2014 ⚐

- That is the old joke: " Had my brain washed and now I can't do a thing with it." Dec 20, 2014 ⚐
- Right. The sequel to Shades of Grey ought to be Shades of Skin. People are multi-colored & this country brainwashed into see only two colors Dec 20, 2014 ⚐
- Why do black women read the most? My guess 70% single. Lots of time, black men scare, or in jail, or can't support a family: race jailing's. Dec 20, 2014 ⚐
- Black women read the most? Some of u doubted that. Here is the citation: http://t.co/zClsck8CwC Dec 20, 2014 ⚐
- I did read Shades of Grey & what? Only in fantasy? which the money or the treatment or both. Men are thinking: do u take food stamps? Dec 20, 2014 ⚐
- You know who reads the most in this country? Black single women. Smoke that. Dec 20, 2014 ⚐
- Motto: some cops next year: Create a felon, get paid. Honest this is what they are being told by Ferguson Dir. of Finance: see link below. Dec 20, 2014 ⚐
- "Nothing more dismaying than a sincerely ignorant debater suggesting that you go read a book." Dec 20, 2014 ⚐

- Is Crayola still issuing "flesh colored" crayons?" Need some "Carmel" in there. Dec 20, 2014
- My favorite quote of the year? "Hard to arrest an idea, but damn they sure love trying." Dec 20, 2014
- "Hard to arrest an idea" Dec 20, 2014
- Every dictator takes away your freedom claiming it is protecting you or for homeland security and shut up or u are a traitor. "Sup?" Dec 20, 2014
- Imagine some conservative congress-crazy creeping in my bedroom saying I can't use birth control or condoms waving some law? Alien abduction. Dec 20, 2014
- Dictator: "Let's make breathing illegal without a permit, or state issue equipment; then we got them." Dec 20, 2014
- "My problem with freedom-loving conservatives is that they only want that freedom for themselves not for others as well." Dec 20, 2014
- Really why should I have to fear cops, to be sure I do, but don't I pay these their salaries, aren't they responsible to us?. Ok forget it. Dec 19, 2014
- Every dictatorial government surveilles: makes everything illegal, they want a big fat net to drag every citizen in and jail's if need be. Dec 19, 2014

- "Society has made nearly everything illegal, even what u do in the privacy of your own home; empowers cops; they then selective enforce laws" Dec 19, 2014 ⚑
- Well, my view: Life is what u are willing to see, expect to see and what after that u are willing to act upon. Dec 19, 2014 ⚑
- They have made life illegal: every person has broken some law, driving 10 miles over speed limit, drinking underage, teen kissing, all illegal Dec 19, 2014 ⚑
- I mean is u can't understand the whole by studying 2-3 of its pts. These institutions are an integrated whole. Understanding pts not enough. Dec 19, 2014 ⚑
- Individuals in the 21st century are awake in exact proportion as to how many of the dots they connect to & among the institutions named below Dec 19, 2014 ⚑
- No,no.no. If you don't want to take the time to understand the Matrix, you are in the Matrix and that movie ends badly. Dec 19, 2014 ⚑
- What I'm doing? Religion, States, Financial, Social, Media-News, Science, Military-Industrial-Security Education, run the world. !'m on it. Dec 19, 2014 ⚑
- #NYC quote "Change is not a single TV show it is a five year series. Got to see it that way." Dec 19, 2014 ⚑

- Tunein #Radio, best of #2014, #music, #podcasts, #news, all that. http://t.co/2v2jpyQehy Dec 19, 2014
- Elites are not just the rich, they are those who have institutional power and wealth, i.e. generals, bureaucrats, CIA? Dec 19, 2014
- "Fixing America" part two http://t.co/x6j4VVV1qF & part 3 http://t.co/Wc7Hhuo9CV pt4 http://t.co/2yh0O fMBBQ pt5 http://t.co/uGHOjWwyLK Dec 19, 2014
- The irony is that elites which all through our history divided us in class, race and color, is by its excesses forcing us to join and unite. Dec 19, 2014
- "Dystopia" http://t.co/H7TE1yJX5e Dec 19, 2014
- Underclasses? It's retail & service workers, students, the blacks, adjunct professors, browns, poor whites, women, all looking for change. Dec 19, 2014
- My thought? Time to plan and think: time to organize: time to roll off the couch. Dec 19, 2014
- One of the best shows on #Ferguson #blacklivesmatter #icantbreathe #ericgarner http://t.co/Hq7h6auEsB Dec 19, 2014
- One of the best new political satire shows #Ferguson #ICantBreathe #EricGarner

#nycprotest
#blacklivesmatter http://t.co/PSqkG7fDPS Dec 19, 2014

- Family of john #crawford to file lawsuit against #Walmart #blacklivesmatter #EricGarner # protests
  #berkeleyprotests http://t.co/WXQLGke8jG Dec 19, 2014

- Electronic watchdog group suit against NSA and ATT at decision point?
  at http://t.co/i3ZfJ9ndAp Dec 19, 2014

- Most powerful photos from #Ferguson http://t.co/QGxmc1Tpkg Dec 19, 2014

- Law enforcement most obese? http://t.co/xxLbqguqWe Dec 19, 2014

- The Black Holocaust #Ferguson #BlackLivesMatter blackOffenders Continue To Pay For Their
  Crimes http://t.co/d5VKNRJU5a via @blackvoices Dec 19, 2014

- Injustice Facts @injustice 516,000 professors in the U.S, only 1 has spoken openly against the 'War on Terror', expelled & career destroyed. Dec 19, 2014

- Hear this: "Every government in history has one goal: control over the population, even as they claim that this is not true." Dec 19, 2014

- Hey I have many degrees: this fight is one my soul insists upon, not for race but for humanity.

If u don't get that u aren't going to get me Dec 19, 2014 ⬚

- Too much of what goes for intellect these days is smoke and mirrors: u don't understand what I am saying, cause I write from my soul: not. Dec 19, 2014 ⬚
- "Passion precedes all true intellect." Dec 19, 2014 ⬚
- Know that song "I'm all about that bass" NASA interns did a parody. I think someone should do one "I'm all about that race." and see 'sup' Dec 19, 2014 ⬚
- Being only a "head" person means u lack #art, #dance, #poetry, #love, #empathy, true #sex, #vision and that sometimes makes you a #zombie. Dec 19, 2014 ⬚
- Well in a serious conflict u have to have to understand your neighbors getting together, working together is your best hope. Dec 19, 2014 ⬚
- I'm saying that modern government has become like the ex: about power, money, control, trashing u, not taking blame, getting pp on their side. Duh Dec 19, 2014 ⬚
- 3rd great photo message: https://t.co/AYAtQoSEqC #Ferguson , #ICantBreathe #MillionsMarchNYC #EricGarner #BlackLivesMatter Dec 19, 2014 ⬚

- Another great photo message https://t.co/kaYUbU50hd Dec 19, 2014 ⚡
- Great photo message https://t.co/CrXI3qwL2t Dec 19, 2014 ⚡
- Pardon me: Sad to say that most whites automatically assume most repressive laws are aimed at "them" Wake up. Not anymore. Dec 19, 2014 ⚡
- We have a country where everything has been criminalized which gives cops the right to cops to stop, search, confront, beat and jail. U too. Dec 19, 2014 ⚡
- Ok, last time: white skin has protected u in the past, privileged u, but not anymore dude. U have been suckered: now it's clear if u look. Dec 19, 2014 ⚡
- Summary demand; Get the tanks out of my neighborhood, disarm them. Dec 19, 2014 ⚡
- Well I'm saying that whites don't yet understand that elites don't really care about color when their power is at stake. They'll do u in too Dec 19, 2014 ⚡
- Wise now mistrust our government: Not just about blacks; we have an entire militarized police army in place which can be used against w's and b's Dec 18, 2014 ⚡
- It's downright shameful judges preach "rule of law;" is that cops, lawyers, & judges? Whatever

happened to rule by consent of the governed? Dec 18, 2014 ⊡

- #NYC quote "Put me in a part-time job and all does is give me more protest time." Dec 18, 2014 ⊡
- It's crazy in US to preach law and order during protests, while tolerating total corruption among police, corruption abroad and corrupt banks Dec 18, 2014 ⊡
- "Just because you make corruption and racism legal doesn't make it right, and doesn't mean I can't protest and do civil disobedience." Dec 18, 2014 ⊡
- Simple point this is institutionalized corruption. Sure not all cops but the ones that don't protect the ones that do behind wall of silence Dec 18, 2014 ⊡
- They routinely impound your car, hundreds of dollars to get it out. This is clearly a racket. #Ferguson, #ICantBreathe #EricGarner #protest Dec 18, 2014 ⊡
- Hell there much more than traffic & shakedowns, cops can do civil forfeiture, that is claim drugs & take my car, use it to pay own salaries. Dec 18, 2014 ⊡
- To be clear I am not against big government I am against big government captured by corporations rather than being run by the people. Dec 18, 2014 ⊡

- Here is the best #finance show on the net. #Ferguson 15% plan discussed among other topics. http://t.co/8t52iLDQWq Dec 18, 2014
- Below applies to most cities large & small. Preying upon the poor has now become so institutionalized these people positively depend upon it Dec 18, 2014
- Here is link to #Ferguson plan to increase traffic fines #BlackLivesMatter #berkeleyprotests #ICantBreathe http://t.co/izjRZbkKn5 Dec 18, 2014
- Unbelievable: #Ferguson Director of Finances says traffic fines must increase 15% in 2015 to make up 1m $ shortfall. U kidding me? Mo riots? Dec 18, 2014
- Congress gave banks rights to gamble with your money, means retirement is being stolen, 0 interest rates on savings, ATM limit withdrawals Dec 18, 2014
- #NYC The Billion Dollar Stop and Frisk business http://t.co/mMtqR3rsUs Dec 18, 2014
- #NYC Shame in the Numbers: NYC made a BILLION $$ in traffic fines in the last 10 funded by Stop and Frisk as the tip of the spear. Link next Dec 18, 2014
- Supreme Court? I think those black robes are actually white and the hoods are hidden underneath the table. Dec 18, 2014

- Racial discrimination in housing, in employment, the justice system is protected by the US Supreme ct. have to prove "intent' Can't be done Dec 18, 2014
- If the Feds are spending all the money on war, local whites have turned to cops, traffic courts, even meter maids to make up the missing $$ Dec 18, 2014
- Sorry my friend, been at demonstrations & seen who gets arrested & charged & felonies and who get a misdemeanor. Ferguson #EricGarner Dec 18, 2014
- #NYC quote 640 THOUSAND Stop and Frisks in NYC: 87% blacks and browns. Sounds like cops are using that Israeli training in the ghetto. Dec 18, 2014
- This: cops are on street looking to earn their own salaries with an arrest, & they do 'cause they can get away with it in the ghetto and do. Dec 18, 2014
- Ok, look at this: "crack" arrests waged in black neighborhoods, cocaine arrests, a white drug, very few arrests. Both are the same drug. Dec 18, 2014
- Look my view is this systematized system preying upon the poor, is evil, slow genocide, shameful & is offensive to any fair-minded person. Dec 18, 2014

- Lots of data for the above claim about drugs. If you want links to the data, DM me. Dec 18, 2014 ₪
- Sorry, whites use drugs at same rate as blacks, yet don't go to jail, cops are in the ghetto with jail and traffic quotas. Dec 18, 2014 ₪
- The War on Drugs has been a war on African Americans: sent to jail for minor drug offences;grass.Traffic plus "war on drugs" used by cops. Dec 18, 2014 ₪
- Debtor prison is real NPR REPORT. We gain nothing if this not fixed http://t.co/1nmx48X84g Dec 18, 2014 ₪
- Jailed for traffic fines. An example http://t.co/53nW21i5YP Dec 18, 2014 ₪
- The courts are virtual debtor's prisons, extracting fines and fees from poor drivers to fund local governments, police, judges, lawyers DMV. Dec 18, 2014 ₪
- Traffic court: make people poor: and keeps them poor-jail.. #Ferguson #blacklivesmatter #berkeleyprotests http://t.co/1rmOSVCTBq Dec 18, 2014 ₪
- Second graders join protest. #Ferguson https://t.co/AR3AWBjrUJ Dec 18, 2014 ₪
- Cuts to local welfare schemes xmas present to loan sharks' http://t.co/84KzxDcqcU Same here

US. JP Morgan & banks own payday loan places. Dec 18, 2014

- FBI Probes Possible Lynching of Lynching of North Carolina Teen? FBI Probe. #blacklivesmatter http://t.co/TyybaCSJzN via @democracynow Dec 18, 2014
- If the Chinese are forced to choose between R and us they stop loaning us money and barter oil with R. Decision made already BRIC Dec 18, 2014
- Best #political humor 2014 http://t.co/dtNcfYfyPH Dec 18, 2014
- Family of 17 year old black teen says he was lynched. #ICantBreathe #EricGarner #BlackLivesMatter #Ferguson #berkeleyprotests Dec 18, 2014
- The prison industrial system profits from locking blacks up and filling prison beds. #Ferguson #blacklivesmatter https://t.co/Oe5OKLnRCT Dec 18, 2014
- Most of u are saying boycotting the Rams game is too risky, alienate football fans: a call being made by a guy no one knows? Dec 17, 2014
- Plan for action Sunday for NFL Rams-Cowboy game SL Good idea? Bad idea? See #video #Ferguson #BlackLivesMatter at: http://t.co/7jKYTOpiPY Dec 17, 2014

- How #Twitter forced the nation to pay attention to police brutality: #Ferguson #ICantBreathe #BlackLivesMatter #Berkeley #MillionsMarchNYC Dec 17, 2014
- Why can't the cops arrest the people breaking windows, that's their job, not tear-gas the whole crowd, that is not policing its suppression. Dec 17, 2014
- The old think, the young lead. Been that way for centuries. Dec 17, 2014
- I'm saying I will not let anyone dictate to me who to love, who to hate, who to kill or maim or how to view others. I'm from Chicago. Dec 17, 2014
- Don't let"em divide you, discourage u, jail u, if avoidable, intimidate u, confuse u, distract u, propagandize u, fear others, monetize u. Dec 17, 2014
- "Our lives begin to end the day we become silent about things that matter" MLK Jr: http://t.co/trCgBK7CXI #ShutItDown http://t.co/LoHWctAdFC Dec 17, 2014
- #shutitdown all across the nation today. #Ferguson #BlackLivesMatter #ICantBreathe #berkeleyprotests #protest #MillionsMarchNYC Dec 17, 2014
- "The idea that we can't live together in peace on this planet is a myth perpetuated by those who benefit from war." Dec 17, 2014

- "Ideology is a serious disease resulting from a prolonged exposure to idiots." Dec 17, 2014 🖉
- My nomination for person of the year? The citizen blogger, journalist, organizer, reacher-outer across race, class, country, & ideologies. Dec 17, 2014 🖉
- Many agendas out there, few real meetings-of mind. Lots of shouting little real hearing or comprehension. Wisdom reduced to sound bites-140 Dec 17, 2014 🖉
- Objective Media? All have an agenda. Mark Twain: If you tune in-read ur misinformed, if u do not ur uninformed about today's propaganda. Dec 17, 2014 🖉
- If it rains one more time just before a planned demonstration here on the coast, my paranoia is cured. Dec 17, 2014 🖉
- Anger, most times, occurs when your knickers are too tight and u think someone else did it. Dec 17, 2014 🖉
- "Sarcasm is the deep disappointment accompanying a Truth no one else acknowledges." Dec 17, 2014 🖉
- If you think there is nothing wrong in this world for others, you have to definitely, positively get off the drugs. Dec 17, 2014 🖉
- Create an entire underclass: students, the poor, immigrants. Vets, white poor, blacks, women, browns, Asians & they'll stay in the streets. Dec 17, 2014 🖉

- U know amazes me how people refuse to get on the Train of History and then wonder why things remain the same: "White Silence: W/h complicity Dec 17, 2014 ⌐
- Great photo-message #berkeleyprotests http://t.co/TqSLC34Tky Dec 17, 2014 ⌐
- Brooklyn lawyer die-in #MillionsMarchNYC #icantbreathe #ericgarner ##blacklivesmatter http://t.co/Nq5Fkv1BnT Dec 17, 2014 ⌐
- Uproar at Berkeley city council meeting here at: http://t.co/yApijlCa6a #berkeleyprotests # protests #blacklivesmatter #Ferguson Dec 17, 2014 ⌐
- Jews for peace .#icantbreathe. #Ferguson #blacklivesmatter http://t.co/8nBrKdAYn1 Dec 17, 2014 ⌐
- #fox news with all their investigative reporters after repeating the "lying" witness version of #Ferguson would recant story. Just joking. Dec 17, 2014 ⌐
- More #video on #Ferguson "lying" witness. http://t.co/u0MAr657V2 #ICantBreathe #blacklivesmatter #ericgarner #berkeleyprotests # Dec 17, 2014 ⌐
- Lawyers in several cities to stage "die-in" today #Ferguson #blacklivesmatter # protests #ICantBreathe http://t.co/aelbeaQXjc Dec 17, 2014 ⌐

- My view? "None so diligent as those trying not to see what is right before them." Dec 17, 2014 🔗
- The ultimate guide to who's who in American media. Best I have seen. http://t.co/ImOJbCTzQc Dec 17, 2014 🔗
- Slate article on #Ferguson "lying" witness at: http://t.co/nr92N47ywl Dec 17, 2014 🔗
- Daily News article on #Ferguson lying witness At: http://t.co/IS0acsb9Lp #Ferguson #ICantBreathe #EricGarner #berkeleyprotests Dec 17, 2014 🔗
- @twitsanon Ok thxs. Dec 17, 2014 🔗
- 10 cents to a dollar national press will ignore this false witness story. #Ferguson, #ICantBreathe #BlackLivesMatter please RT and forward. Dec 16, 2014 🔗
- Somebody ought to go jail, lose their job or both. Let's see what happens. Dec 16, 2014 🔗
- This is the article about the lying witness. #Ferguson, #BlackLivesMatter http://t.co/D7HRN6vnZl Dec 16, 2014 🔗
- Key witness in Brown case admits to lying. #Ferguson #BlackLivesMatter #EricGarner #MillionsMarchNYC #protest At: http://t.co/D7HRN6vnZl Dec 16, 2014 🔗
- #NYC In light of key witness admitting to lying #Ferguson DA should resign? #ICantBreathe

#BlackLivesMatter #berkeleyprotests #EricGarner Dec 16, 2014 ⊠

- Key witness in Brown shooting (he pummeled Wilson & charged like football player) admits to lying. #Ferguson #ICantBreathe #BlackLivesMatter Dec 16, 2014 ⊠
- The Middle Class in Trouble in the United States? The #Washington Post examines why. http://t.co/rqQ9EduHQ3 Dec 16, 2014 ⊠
- PBS: The top ten stories of 2014 at: http://t.co/s5UVGqPa3X Dec 16, 2014 ⊠
- The Year in #Twitter https://t.co/tk6l1QCZaM Dec 16, 2014 ⊠
- # at: https://t.co/zrLi8BbgVo Dec 16, 2014 ⊠
- Our weekly newspaper: UK EDITION # Newspaper at: https://t.co/P2ZNOkBZjM Dec 16, 2014 ⊠
- Beware: CIA. FBI, your ex. celebrities all edit, change, shade Wikipedia pages? Is nothing sacred? Dec 16, 2014 ⊠
- Beware: Congressional staffers caught editing, changing, shading Wikipedia pages? Is nothing sacred? But more: government does it all the time. Dec 16, 2014 ⊠
- The desperate and getting desperater plight of the Millennials. Is this is what is fueling protests? Dec 16, 2014 ⊠
- Why is the press so shocked by broken windows at home all the while tolerating

unspeakable torture at home; & horrible violence abroad. Dec 16, 2014

- Believe none of what u read in the press, no government handout, none of TV, trust in your own critical thinking, always ask why & why & why again Dec 16, 2014

- #NYC Beware: Cops can use your social media photos and comments as evidence of crimes, lewd behavior, drug use etc. Dec 16, 2014

- Most of the big countries love wars & conflict cause they get to sell arms to both sides & then swoop in stealing resources "helping" Dec 16, 2014

- Previous 3k #tweets All my #Tweets http://t.co/oaYQj2HLYd. Sign and then search using my handle @lnnie Dec 16, 2014

- #NYC quote "Trust? No, no, no, this is about Cease and Desist." Dec 16, 2014

- #NYC quote "Shooting people is not dialogue." Dec 16, 2014

- @Lnnie That's why the police should not be armed, as in the UK. Offer a job with a gun, you get applicants who want guns Dec 16, 2014

- #NYC quote "A cop with a gun and an attitude is a danger to everyone." Dec 16, 2014

- Hating people who hate saps your energy, diverts u from moving ahead and gives u acne. Dec 16, 2014 &
- #NYC quote "Some want change as long as u don't have to do anything differently." Dec 16, 2014 &
- Two #US #wars cost 3 trillion - borrowed money http://t.co/0nveedO42e Dec 16, 2014 &
- Whites a minority in US population by 2044? US Census Data. http://t.co/zUfctYMXiZ Dec 16, 2014 &
- #Russia headed toward recession? http://t.co/KSX41v0U4w Dec 16, 2014 &
- #blacklivesmatter #Ferguson #ICantBreathe #HandsUpWalkout #berkeleyprotests. http://t.co/WAkEuNpw7u Dec 16, 2014 &
- The three things the powers that be do not want you to have is information, a job, and hope. Any two will do. Dec 16, 2014 &
- Protests continue nationwide. "Complacency is Consent". #berkeleyprotests #BlackLivesMatter #ICantBreathe https://t.co/7BsXfNUmXn Dec 16, 2014 &
- Hey spirits don't have an age, nor does love, nor does desire, so there. Shut down the TV propaganda. Dec 16, 2014 &

- What small towns and large got what in military equipment and why, oh why? http://t.co/FexbTLsVGD Dec 15, 2014 ☍
- #Elizabeth Warren not giving up. Challenging Democratic Liberals, wall street. http://t.co/Nje7FG5tb0 Dec 15, 2014 ☍
- Huh? What if I am wrong? So, what if I am wrong? Is it a crime? If so the jails will fill up with politicians. Dec 15, 2014 ☍
- Actually more countries have joined BRIC. If they fund it, the dollar will go bye, bye if we move to swap economics, barter Dec 15, 2014 ☍
- Well the cynical point, (which I am not recommending) is demonstrations cost average of 100,000 day. Maybe cost will get folks to change Dec 15, 2014 ☍
- Proposed Illinois law makes it illegal felony to eavesdrop on cops or government officials? http://t.co/YtzYDQNJ1t #Ferguson, #ICantBreathe Dec 15, 2014 ☍
- #Lennon Lacy 17 yr. old black male found hung last Aug. Question: Suicide or Lynching? FBI involved #BlueLivesMatter http://t.co/h83HsrT1a2 Dec 15, 2014 ☍
- Bad news for #Florida? #climate change Coming Sooner Rather than Later? http://t.co/7P1BvPxDUL Dec 15, 2014 ☍

- Public Housing Patrols: Stop and Frisk with a twist #ICantBreathe #BlackLivesMatter #Ferguson #HandsUpDontShoot at: http://t.co/GISjdM5556 Dec 15, 2014
- If u don't read the newspaper u are uninformed. If u do read the newspaper u are misinformed. Mark Twain. Dec 15, 2014
- @loreleibrown44 http://t.co/kaOaXGVnmf Dec 15, 2014
- So much rain in northern California beginning to wonder if Feds have learned how to seed clouds to make rain. Dec 15, 2014
- Time lapse video of Millions March NYC (Time Lapse): http://t.co/mvA830r8KF #MillionsMarch NYC #blacklivesmatter#ericgarner #berkeleyprotests Dec 15, 2014
- #Energy firms face bankruptcy http://t.co/uzH0PjoWMN Dec 15, 2014
- Our weekly newspaper 12/15/14 http://t.co/OkiVjTuVtU #blacklivesmatter #Ferguson #ICantBreathe Dec 15, 2014
- Sexual harassment 'part of daily life' for young girls – study — RT UK http://t.co/MnPRH7GMUm Dec 15, 2014
- Derivatives is the practice, for example, of selling the same mortgage cash flow 400 times. Fraud! Total D's 1 quardrillion Tot worldGNP 75t Dec 15, 2014

- The Novel Title on Finance Sector? "A Surplus of Crooks" Dec 15, 2014 🖉
- Solutions to world finances: denounce debt: bitcoin; exit EU zone; end fiat currency; BRIC; Barter; Coops-Devolution, Nationalize banks duh Dec 15, 2014 🖉
- Don't let'em divide u by race, class-country, distracts: stop the jailing, stay peaceful, careful. ICantBreathe #berkeleyprotests #Berkeley Dec 14, 2014 🖉
- Yes, I saying, don't let'em divide you by race, class or country, don't let'em distract u, stop the jailing, stay peaceful, be careful. Dec 14, 2014 🖉
- Funny on the web: "I wasn't planning on going on a run today, but those cops came out of nowhere.". Dec 14, 2014 🖉
- I was happy at all the followers. But, sadly, most of them were cops. Dec 14, 2014 🖉
- Inflaming racial divisions has been the at the heart soul of American politics since the very beginning. These effigies may be an example. Dec 14, 2014 🖉
- Former female PM embroiled in paternity suit. Satan denies paternity. Dec 14, 2014 🖉
- Three lynched #effigies found at UC Berkeley #ICantBreathe #BlackLivesMatter #berkeleyprotests http://t.co/mPMACrhqjf Dec 14, 2014 🖉

- Satan refuses to run for Congress and says if elected he "will not serve." Cites corruption. Dec 14, 2014 🔗
- #nyt "Is It Bad Enough Yet?" At: http://t.co/W1eTQ41nA5 "True citizenship is people continually protesting" T. Jefferson Dec 14, 2014 🔗
- Congress hides huge union pension cuts in the dead of night spending bill, say critics. At: http://t.co/OpUO50SahX Dec 14, 2014 🔗
- School disciple for #girls differs by race? #Ferguson #ICantBreathe #EricGarner #HandsUpWalkout #protests http://t.co/wAkxVlMJyK Dec 14, 2014 🔗
- All my Tweets: use twitter handle @lnnie 'get tweets' ##icantbreathe #BlackLivesMatter #ericgarner #berkeleyprotests http://t.co/SzFioH57gu Dec 14, 2014 🔗
- All my #Tweets http://t.co/oaYQj2HLYd Dec 14, 2014 🔗
- #NYC quote: "Excuse me officer do u really need the tank? Dec 14, 2014 🔗
- Read: Michelle Alexander "The New Jim Crow" #ICantBreathe #BlackLivesMatter #ericgarner #HandsUpWalkout #berkeleyprotests #MillionsMarchNYC Dec 14, 2014 🔗

- #NYC quote "I have been misinformed and miseducated. I am not going back." Dec 14, 2014
- "Freedom, Justice, and Equality" at http://t.co/8qieRMK5EL Dec 14, 2014
- What I mean is democracy is a means; freedom is an outcome. One without the other is meaningless. Dec 14, 2014
- Plan? If the population is jobless, dependent on government handouts, u have neither democracy nor freedom. Don't even have to offer them. Dec 14, 2014
- I am always amazed at how populations take so long to see clearly what are massive financial crimes. Dec 14, 2014
- "Let's Talk About #Race: What are the facts? #ICantBreathe #blacklivesmatter At: http://t.co/85FxOvDo8F Dec 14, 2014
- @sn0wba111 But to pay for bail out they are told reduced pensions joblessness sell country assets savings gone. Hidden taxes all. Dec 14, 2014
- "Politics" at http://t.co/gqvGnUqel5 Dec 14, 2014
- #Haitian Prime minister forced to resign in face of antigovernment protests. http://t.co/fDaQVz7Eqg Dec 14, 2014

- #EU an austerity disaster: impoverishing middle class? http://t.co/JNmiK1Tfhe Dec 14, 2014 🖉
- Will there be prosecutions in the wake of CIA report? Not likely some say.
  At: http://t.co/B38kVfjvB4 Dec 14, 2014 🖉
- #Feds want to search #Facebook data http://t.co/ZLAgISke7I Dec 14, 2014 🖉
- National # protests #icantbreathe #blacklivesmatter #Ferguson #HandsUpDontShoot #ericgarner berkeleyprotests http://t.co/EzjoSdzPSY Dec 14, 2014 🖉
- Thousands protest in Boston. #icantbreathe #berkeleyprotests #Ferguson #blacklivesmatter http://t.co/Ea0hLcDhbt Dec 14, 2014 🖉
- Some say slavery and jail the same. Donno. My thought: both horrendous. But some slaves got free. Not with those in jail. Both bad though. Dec 14, 2014 🖉
- More #videos #photos Huff Post #MillionsMarchNYC at: http://t.co/OnhpokAurl Dec 14, 2014 🖉
- Sure, could be a frat prank. Don't know. We'll see if anything is found out. Dec 14, 2014 🖉
- The Associated Press, quoting Berkeley spokeswoman Amy Hamaoui, reported the effigies were found in two prominent areas of the campus. Dec 14, 2014 🖉

- Why? These kids sense that for their generation this is maybe their last chance to make a break for freedom. They are taking it. Dec 14, 2014 🔗
- Threaten somebody's job, income, status, or expose them is what it usually takes to get change. Open the jails & the "justice" system falls. Dec 14, 2014 🔗
- More blacks in jail than were enslaved in 1864. Call it progress if you want to, at least the slaves were not in jail. Dec 14, 2014 🔗
- Look, DA's judges, cops, public defenders, DMV, lawyers, small towns, courts, all depend upon tickets, warrants, jail for their income. Duh. Dec 14, 2014 🔗
- Once they are locked away it is too easy to forget them, and they count on that. Making millions off the locked up. Dec 14, 2014 🔗
- My recommendation: Stop the non-violent-crime to-jail-treadmill, free a million people. That is the million people freed march. Go for that. Dec 14, 2014 🔗
- The path to "yes" is just as easy as the path to "no." Yes, really. Wouldn't you agree? Dec 14, 2014 🔗
- All I am saying is that it is a poor archer that only has one arrow in the quiver. Dec 14, 2014 🔗

- #NYC quote "They are going to try to out wait us. No chance. Half of us are already waiters." Dec 14, 2014 🔗
- What's this finance stuff & wall street & the 1.1 trillion dollar spending bill about? Answer: your future and they just ripped it off. Dec 14, 2014 🔗
- What I like about our young people in the streets? They were not listening when people told them nothing could be done. Dec 14, 2014 🔗
- Trusting reps and dems is like swimming with crocodiles. It can be done. Not. Dec 14, 2014 🔗
- #WallStreet street guts the #Dodd Frank reform bill. Back to the good old days. http://t.co/se7BxePLSa Dec 14, 2014 🔗
- What'd I mean? Some leaders tell u what they think. Young people out there told what happened to them & how that felt. "Leaders" can't do that Dec 13, 2014 🔗
- https://t.co/VFkTUHq4OF photos, tweets, messages Dec 13, 2014 🔗
- Regina Antonia Calca and 126 others follow @Jmoon @Jmoon901 5m5 minutes ago #Berkeley young #protesters marching up Broadway Dec 13, 2014 🔗
- Sure, but it is 2:30 here on the west coast, demonstrations just getting started. Dec 13, 2014 🔗

- Michael Green @green4h2o 1h 1 hour ago "Try not to become a man of success, but rather try to become a man of value." #quote Albert Einstein Dec 13, 2014 ⮌
- A lot of "national leaders" tried for the mike. Young people out there for 120 days demanded to speak & they did speak. They were for real. Dec 13, 2014 ⮌
- Police ALWAYS minimize the number of people in demonstrations Dec 13, 2014 ⮌
- Young #Ferguson interviewed. #ICantBreathe #MillionsMarchNYC #ICantBreathe #BlackLivesMatter #EricGarner http://t.co/bivOJxZ5CM Dec 13, 2014 ⮌
- @OccupyWallStNYC Arrested at #MillionsMarchNYC call the NYC National Lawyers Guild hotline 212-679-6018, w/names + locs/times of arrests Dec 13, 2014 ⮌
- If #MillionsMarchNYC is really 30+ blocks long, that's 800K square feet. At one person per 10 square feet, that'd be 80,000 people. Dec 13, 2014 ⮌
- #MillionsMarchNYC #photos, tweets, and hashtag stories. https://t.co/UfAaUGdgBF Dec 13, 2014 ⮌
- Police presence at #MillionsMarchNYC is huge. All peaceful and very organized so far #EricGarner

#ICantBreathe http://t.co/onDPnAlLsB Dec 13, 2014 🖉

- But can't help wonder: a march of 10,000. Again capital police show restraint No problem. #ICantBreathe #BlackLivesMatter #EricGarner Dec 13, 2014 🖉
- Protesters in DC, #Video #ICantBreathe #Ferguson #BlackLivesMatter #HandsUpDontShoot #EricGarner Protesters in DC, http://t.co/69HitEm4so Dec 13, 2014 🖉
- Sure but he gets 1 million but the bill at Ferguson: 1.5 million police & national guard, 40m in lawsuits for police conduct. Who pays that? Dec 13, 2014 🖉
- Darren Wilson walks away with one million dollars: paid interviews and "donations" Dec 13, 2014 🖉
- #magicjohnson supports protesters at: http://t.co/xUoeNEgiy2 #Ferguson #BlackLivesMatter Dec 13, 2014 🖉
- International coverage of protests: #ICantBreathe #BlackLivesMatter At: https://t.co/ElPWkKzOeV Dec 13, 2014 🖉
- Celebrities support #ICantBreathe at: http://t.co/OMXRTIdH8P #Ferguson #KobeBryant Dec 13, 2014 🖉
- #NYC quote: Why after every shooting they always rush the cop point of view out but never witnesses, the victim's family. Why that? Dec 13, 2014 🖉

- Live Network TV coverage of the protests at:https://t.co/kaQF10w7R9 … #BlackLivesMatter #ICantBreathe #protest #EricGarner Dec 13, 2014 ⬀
- #Video of protests #Ferguson https://t.co/oBWq89OOpM Dec 13, 2014 ⬀
- http://t.co/l5s6vd9tS7 Dec 13, 2014 ⬀
- Goal: Decriminalize non-violent offences. That will stop the pipeline to jail. #Ferguson #ICantBreathe #BlackLivesMatter #berkeleyprotests Dec 13, 2014 ⬀
- protests on internet radioat: http://t.co/zMMUyW4UYi Berk, &at http://t.co/laDWEV7ebV DC http://t.co/6tP2 OsOjTr useTunein radio free d/load Dec 13, 2014 ⬀
- #HandsupGunsDown Sums it up.#ICantBreathe #berkeleyprotests #BlackLivesMatter #EricGarner Dec 13, 2014 ⬀
- Live radio coverage of national protests on internet radio at: http://t.co/zMMUyW4UYi Berkeley, & at http://t.co/laDWEV7ebV Washington DC Dec 13, 2014 ⬀
- @CoilaHodges There will be a #BlackLivesMatter march Bancroft & Telegraph noon; might join #MillionsMarch in Oakland at 2 #berkeleyprotests Dec 13, 2014 ⬀

- #Elizabeth Warren fiery speech See her cspan video http://t.co/a3TNNsqTjL Dec 13, 2014 🔗
- See here cspan video http://t.co/a3TNNsqTjL Dec 13, 2014 🔗
- Millions March #NYC #ICantBreathe #HandsUpDontShoot #Ferguson #blacklivesmatter http://t.co/pzPML7ckCx Dec 13, 2014 🔗
- Protests-Breaking the rules? https://t.co/VrxTH0kT2U Dec 13, 2014 🔗
- #icantbreathe playlist for event http://t.co/v8qgD4kZSD Dec 13, 2014 🔗
- NFL Cheerleaders sue owners http://t.co/XVYTIUP43U Dec 13, 2014 🔗
- Protest songs go viral #icantbreathe #blacklivesmatter #Ferguson #HandsUpDontShoot #Berkeley http://t.co/lXhWPWsW0G Dec 13, 2014 🔗
- Millions March http://t.co/qoZLO01Z7i Dec 13, 2014 🔗
- 13 #Senators voted against the just passed #Defense Bill. Their individual statements as to why. At:http://t.co/oqXOpNCazN Dec 13, 2014 🔗
- Tonite: Senate passes defense bill 89-11: Spending bill set for next week http://t.co/x9iXLOQMFj Dec 13, 2014 🔗

- Looks like #ElizabethWarren Warren is warming up for the race in 2016. At: http://t.co/1MYP0u051r Dec 13, 2014 ⬚
- My secret to happiness: If I can't have it; I don't want it; if I don't need it; I don't want it. If I can have it later, I can wait. Dec 13, 2014 ⬚
- Italy workers strike out against austerity.43% unemployment for under 25's at: http://t.co/pZyjPiVDLW Dec 13, 2014 ⬚
- So many women write me saying, marrying a rich man is its own trap. U end up hankering for death, revenge, affairs, & understanding. Dec 13, 2014 ⬚
- If u dream a lot about money, fame, beauty, power, revenge, and having more, more, more, you drank the Kool-Aid. Dec 13, 2014 ⬚
- Don't have to be superman, super handsome, super beautiful, super smart, super-rich to be morally right. Dec 13, 2014 ⬚
- You can grow up learning love just yourself, or yourself & only your own, or yourself, your own & others too. These will determine your life Dec 13, 2014 ⬚
- Older people can be bitchy, true. But think how much crap they have seen in their lives, and try to be understanding. Ask'em about it. Dec 13, 2014 ⬚
- Didn't like getting older, didn't expect to reach 30, 40 was crazy, 50 was busy, after that

started getting younger 'cause 100 was in sight Dec 13, 2014

- Got to have something more to look forward to other than that next bargain, that next consumable. Besides where did u learn to rely upon that? Dec 13, 2014
- Ok, but if you can't see beyond skin, you will be hating your own when it wrinkles up. Dec 13, 2014
- My grandmother's last words on her death bed. "I don't have time for dying. Got too much to do. Ok, maybe just this one time." A funny lady Dec 12, 2014
- @Missmo1951Jones Funny woman Dec 12, 2014
- Funny from Moms Mabley 70 yrs old. "Don't want no 70 yr old man! Only thing a 70 yr old can do for me: bring me message from a hot 50 yr old Dec 12, 2014
- If you are not a little wild when u are young, gonna look a little silly at 50 trying it out & resentful of the 20 yr olds having fun too Dec 12, 2014
- Well if I had all the answers I would be smarter than I am. Dec 12, 2014
- Well my Dad used to say when you die there'll be two elevators: One says "Up" one says "Down" Figure out which 1's for u before u get there. Dec 12, 2014

- #NYC quote You old people had your chance. U messed up and sold out Now we taking over. Dec 12, 2014 🔗
- Hope not. The day I can no longer be shocked, I get my "New Zombie card. Dec 12, 2014 🔗
- A Living Death" The #Video #aclu #ICantBreathe #EricGarner #BlackLivesMatter #Ferguson #berkeleyprotests https://t.co/x7b56iMdbp Dec 12, 2014 🔗
- Sentenced to a living death? Who are the ones sentenced? See at: https://t.co/2c5mTINze3 Dec 12, 2014 🔗
- 79 percent of 3,278 prisoners serving life wi/to parole were sentenced to die in prison for nonviolent drug crimes. http://t.co/sO7JyROTSc Dec 12, 2014 🔗
- Massive die-in #NYC #ICANTBREATHE http://t.co/zFWH5nNgi9 Dec 12, 2014 🔗
- #TortureReport scandal uk http://t.co/8MRPmtFAOQ Dec 12, 2014 🔗
- Huge protests over education france #berkeleyprotests http://t.co/Hda1BKNGVA Dec 12, 2014 🔗
- 150 congressional staffers walkout #ICantBreathe #BlackLivesMatter #Ferguson #berkeleyprotests

#HandsUpDontShoot http://t.co/tZ3x2sEMuN Dec 12, 2014 ☞

- The only, best & most profound rule in the world is the simple one Jesus enunciated: "Do unto others as you would have done unto you." Dec 12, 2014 ☞
- You know some people only see the light at that moment of their death, but then it's too late to help the living, Don't be one of those. Dec 12, 2014 ☞
- #Einstein powerful words on racism #ICantBreathe #BlackLivesMatter #berkeleyprotests #EricGarner #Ferguson at: http://t.co/sVorp4nyHf Dec 12, 2014 ☞
- The first symptoms of elite abuse among the poor is alcoholism, family abuse, drugs, mental health; the beauty is that poor blame themselves Dec 12, 2014 ☞
- I highly recommend: #authors, #writers #storytelling https://t.co/kXt6MCuG73 Dec 12, 2014 ☞
- Look, the intent of racism is to steal the resources, the labor, the lands, and the wealth of minorities. That ain't hard to see. Dec 12, 2014 ☞
- U can do a lot of things in your head but to succeed you have to do it and do it also with others u love and or respect. Plunge. Dec 12, 2014 ☞

- if all u want to do is to forget the past u are compartmentalizing: cutting off an important part of who u are. Brave-up deal with that past. Dec 12, 2014 ⚐
- Looking forward is not possible wit out looking back. An honest Tomorrow isn't possible without an understanding of Now based on the past Dec 12, 2014 ⚐
- The young take a while to fully understand there is evil in the world, that's why we have religion & fairy tales; breaking the news gently. Dec 12, 2014 ⚐
- Folks economic ups & downs are just elites letting working people create wealth, land, housing, etc. & cheating them out of it; re-taking it. Dec 12, 2014 ⚐
- The powerful always re-write history to glorify themselves, the fearful always try to forget history, their own included; the brave demur. Dec 12, 2014 ⚐
- Black girls getting criminalized and set up for jail time. #ICantBreathe #BlackLivesMatter #Ferguson #EricGarner http://t.co/wAkxVlMJyK Dec 12, 2014 ⚐
- Who needs banks. Peer to Peer Lending is growing. http://t.co/bsuXzfNcXA Dec 12, 2014 ⚐
- Most of us, not just blacks are descended from slaves, indentured servants, poor, peasants,

the raped, the brutalized, the murdered & lepers Dec 12, 2014

- Think about it this way: 99% of most people in the world for 2.5k years have been enslaved by elites. What does that tell u.? Still doing it Dec 12, 2014

- Ok, I am saying all government does this to the people, everywhere, in all of history. Gotta read history. See http://t.co/1nlmgWNRda Dec 12, 2014

- No u want to know whose shoulders does has your property and prosperity derive from? Look back. Dec 12, 2014

- No: saying American prosperity has always been based on: appropriation: lands of the Indians, labor of the slaves, low wage blacks, women. Dec 12, 2014

- Me? Paranoia would have saved millions of lives in pre-war Germany. Dec 12, 2014

- Am I opinionated? Why I think so. "Thinking" is the operative word. Dec 12, 2014

- Well are my solutions? Here are some. "Fixing America" Lots more as well at: http://t.co/5eTdgQjtlU Dec 12, 2014

- Change only comes when you threaten jail, income or someone's job. Fact of life. Dec 12, 2014

- Has the rain stopped. Do wild bears use toilet paper in the woods? Don't think so. Dec 12, 2014

- Well in today's world, u have to be able to walk and chew gum at the same time. Lots of things going on at all times. Dec 12, 2014 ⊡
- Well who has an extra 340k.to give? Ans.The rich. Your 2 dollar donation's ignored. Fat cats buy politicians like slaves in suits. Dec 12, 2014 ⊡
- Why are we in Afghanistan? Afghanistan has the world largest deposit of rare earth minerals, used in your cell phone etc. That why. Dec 12, 2014 ⊡
- Ok pulling the lid off the rain barrel. Dec 12, 2014 ⊡
- Undercover cop pulls gun: http://t.co/LYjDwPco6s #berkeleyprotests Dec 12, 2014 ⊡
- Police overtime in Oakland at: http://t.co/HHmMH0umNn Dec 12, 2014 ⊡
- Has rain stopped? Blub, Blub, glug, glug, #hellastorm #BayAreaStorm Dec 12, 2014 ⊡
- Pictures of Berkeley Storm #hellastorm #BayAreaStorm at: http://t.co/WrSgsuQIrB Dec 11, 2014 ⊡
- When the rains stop. I will send the news by sonar. Dec 11, 2014 ⊡
- Go to Congress: lobby them (I have done this) & there is a hidden sign behind on the wall; "Don't mistake me for someone who really cares" Dec 11, 2014 ⊡

- #BayAreaStorm #hellastorm weather report: Rains expected to end around the 1st of NEVER. Dec 11, 2014 🔗
- Ok my short holiday list: one pair of fins and snorkel and blow pipe. Ain't kidding. Actually did get it once.
  See: http://t.co/raWAXU9Pdu Dec 11, 2014 🔗
- Look you learn over the years to see that nearly everyone is beautiful, if you learn to see their souls. Dec 11, 2014 🔗
- If it rains ONE MORE INCH I'm gonna have a tantrum- and then have some ice cream and chocolate. Dec 11, 2014 🔗
- Freud said that water is associated with sex. If I smoked I would light up right about now.#hellastorm #BayAreaStorm Dec 11, 2014 🔗
- Yes I sure scattered around #fox news are a lot of straw men and dead horses. Dec 11, 2014 🔗
- Thx to @cantata21 "Nothing in the world is more dangerous than sincere ignorance and conscientious stupidity Martin Luther King. Dec 11, 2014 🔗
- Sorry to have to tell you this, but I'm pretty sure STRAWMAN was beaten to death by Fox News about 5 years ago. @FactsMatter @hughcmcbride. Dec 11, 2014 🔗
- #BayAreaStorm #hellastorm Folks: Ark seats cheap. Two pets only! Dec 11, 2014 🔗

- Last time I ask my Indian relatives for the special rain dance. Dec 11, 2014 ⚑
- Just got an idea for a new super-hero STRAWMAN: can suck up lakes, rivers, & big rain storms, preventing mudslides etc. Huh? I've seem worse Dec 11, 2014 ⚑
- Power always goes down in big storms; getting the big light and the carrier pigeons ready. Dec 11, 2014 ⚑
- Lots of people rowing to work today, the one's with absolutely no sense. Dec 11, 2014 ⚑
- No, don't mind debate, but the only way I know u are sincere is if that complaint, opinion has a solution attached. When I say that: silence Dec 11, 2014 ⚑
- I'm saying put 3 rich people in a room: right away they conspire to get more money out of us & to take as much money as possible to the grave Dec 11, 2014 ⚑
- U have 300 people in a business producing the product and get peanuts and a few wealthy owners and shareholders walk off with all the money? Dec 11, 2014 ⚑
- Ur saying the poor what something for nothing: u never ask if the rich born to wealth r getting something for nothing? Did they work for it? Dec 11, 2014 ⚑
- Slow down? Just catching up what has been going on in this country in the last 30 years is a

24/7 job, #Satan has been busy. Dec 11, 2014

- Facts on Security
  Guards: http://t.co/i4obniblrm https://t.co/n36Cy
  8Rr5D Only 12 states require Security Guards
  to report shootings. Dec 11, 2014
- Factoid. 500k police in US but also 1 million
  armed "security guards" Guns, little training, no
  mental health checks. This is a good idea? Dec
  11, 2014
- New bill allows donors to give 1.5m to each
  candidate. Crocodile tears: politicians now get
  big money which they can spend any they
  want. Dec 11, 2014
- Been raining eight inches here. The ark is
  taking on water. #hellastorm
  #BayAreaStorm Dec 11, 2014
- Yes we can, We can change our selves and
  change our minds. But it ain't easy takes work,
  time, vision, and a mule kick. Dec 11, 2014
- "We all get convinced by what we already
  believe." Dec 11, 2014
- I'm saying I don't trust a person who has no
  sense of fun, play, & especially if they don't
  have a sense of humor. Zombies have none of
  these Dec 11, 2014
- More and more I am really beginning to
  see/feel that those in control ARE
  psychopaths. See my article on this
  at:http://t.co/gc65ZmBk0z Dec 11, 2014

- Black men when they get out of prison can't rejoin their family living in Fed sub-subsidized housing. if they do family gets evicted. Why? Dec 11, 2014
- Basic rule, don't leave friends & marchers behind in jail. Get'em help, get'em out. #ICantBreathe #berkeleyprotests #BlackLivesMatter Dec 11, 2014
- The Montgomery Bus Boycott took a year, but started a whole new era. Dec 11, 2014
- #NYC quote: By stander: Why are u marching. Marcher: Why aren't you? Dec 11, 2014
- A country of low wages, living on handouts from the government, repressed in the streets, is not a democracy, nor is it a free country. Dec 11, 2014
- Expose #ALEC #boycott its funders. This group is evil. Even Satan was rejected for membership. See #ALECexposed #BlackLivesMatter Dec 11, 2014
- #CIA the 7 major countries participating in secret jails http://t.co/VKcNFrqJuC Dec 11, 2014
- Police tracking and spying during protests #berkeleyprotests http://t.co/1Ehjc229Su Dec 11, 2014
- #waterprotest Water as a weapon #ICantBreathe http://t.co/eZiMvkcBVm Dec 11, 2014

- #Ferguson the poor neighborhood crisis http://t.co/S5KmafubY1 Dec 11, 2014 ⏍
- #oceans in distress http://t.co/hGQDhX1g8x Dec 11, 2014 ⏍
- #PoliceBrutality problems in the UK http://t.co/wThime9EYK Dec 11, 2014 ⏍
- #NYC #ICantBreathe #berkeleyprotests http://t.co/Vj230DMy7G Dec 11, 2014 ⏍
- #PersonoftheYear of the Year 2014 Runner-Up: Ferguson protesters #Ferguson #blacklivesmatter #TIMEPOY http://t.co/CHjC5SnzMm via @TIME Dec 11, 2014 ⏍
- Why young white #millennials are angry #berkeleyprotests top : / /the http://t.co/QQR0V5gA1o Dec 11, 2014 ⏍
- http://t.co/audxjMigNm Dec 11, 2014 ⏍
- Black congressional staffers to protest. #Icantbreathe #ericgarner http://t.co/HXaMMqxjP2 Dec 11, 2014 ⏍
- The Pill Box Killing of Black Man in Phoenix #ICantBreathe #berkeleyprotests #BlackLivesMatter #Ferguson at: http://t.co/NnndKJam31 Dec 11, 2014 ⏍
- Ok, folks. Remember, Onward! Lift upwards, Don't get Discouraged. Dec 11, 2014 ⏍

- #NYC quote: Marcher: I am deeply angry at what they have allowed to happen to my future. Dec 11, 2014 🔗
- Some whites knew what was happening to blacks in this country; ignored it, now young people stepping up: Appropriate-effects all of us. Dec 11, 2014 🔗
- The young are waking up to the evil and corruption that exists at the top and in virtually all of our institutions. Dec 11, 2014 🔗
- Expose #ALEC #boycott its funders. This group is evil. Even Satan was rejected for membership. Dec 11, 2014 🔗
- If u haven't sat down and talked to some POC in the last few weeks, you are behind. Dec 11, 2014 🔗
- 40 of the 80 American med schools participate in 'die=ins" today. Law schools in the nation join in. Dec 11, 2014 🔗
- UCSF med students conducts "die-in" state black patients die more often than white patients, not an accident. Cite abuses in care, funding. Dec 11, 2014 🔗
- music poetry, reading, community everyday: Today: poetry:http://t.co/wu7pSWy05F & http://t.co/1n9B97orDk & http://t.co/68wEMXO62m Dec 11, 2014 🔗

- #NYC if they are shooting blacks today, u gotta be tons of naive to think they won't shoot u too if u if they decide to. Dec 11, 2014 ⊡
- @EddieGEastcoast A point that. Dec 11, 2014 ⊡
- Why do I use "hell" so much cause that's where Republicans, Wall Street, generals, congress people maintain their residence now & soon to b Dec 11, 2014 ⊡
- Well let me be the first to diagnose this: American hypocrisy is an inbuilt, continuing, deadly disease killing millions home and abroad. Dec 11, 2014 ⊡
- Hey, if 500 white kids a year were being killed by black cops, be honest what would u do? Dec 11, 2014 ⊡
- Are republicans evil? Let's send that to a grand jury of blacks. No need. Answer hell yes. But note they think they are saints. Go figure. Dec 11, 2014 ⊡
- What's in that vaccine food u you kept pushing on me? http://t.co/6k3Ljw73gV Dec 11, 2014 ⊡
- If u have been arrested call National Lawyers Guild Bay Area Hotline: 415-285-1011+ Dec 11, 2014 ⊡
- @tonei thx will post If u need bail, lawyer call National Lawyers Guild Bay Area Hotline: 415-285-1011 occupy has a service too. Dec 11, 2014 ⊡

- It's simple, u don't get to control, violate, incarcerate, kill, mutilate my body cause I a woman, black, brown young, immigrant, poor what. Dec 11, 2014
- Hell we need to know what is in our food, our water, our air, vaccines, our meds, why can't we know these things? Answer: Republicans. Dec 11, 2014
- Well u know Obama has already pardoned himself, bush and Cheney. Swell. Dec 11, 2014
- Information compiled by Open Society Foundations, at least 54 governments cooperated with these CIA activities. http://t.co/Us5EKfTFEv Dec 11, 2014
- Well feels too much like our so called leaders have feet of clay & balls of cotton, (eye balls, I mean, I really just mean eyeballs. Honest. Dec 11, 2014
- McDonald sales r down. Great. Let's put the clown in a Volkswagen and tell him to leave town. Black Friday has and is having an effect. Huh? Dec 11, 2014
- @jessicam1909 Just realizing a lot of this stuff. Dec 11, 2014
- What kind of society would I replace ours with? Sorry when you get rid of a cancer, you don't ask what are u going to replace it with. Dec 11, 2014

- Why am I paying heavy taxes for this heavy surveillance and "boot on the neck" stuff? Dec 11, 2014
- New #Xbox and #PSP? These people wanted to put a secret camera and mike in there to spy on you watching TV and playing #games. #Psychopaths! Dec 11, 2014
- If u brutalize society with manipulated threat after threat some societies will make u dictator just to relieve the stress. Dec 11, 2014
- Surveillance society equals the #ICantBreathe society. Get out of my life. Dec 11, 2014
- You know every oppressive society feels like #ICantBreathe That fits. Dec 11, 2014
- You know Snowden was paid without a college diploma over 100k in security job. That tells you how much money they have to through around. Dec 11, 2014
- They keep telling me how there are protecting me from "terrorists" Sorry you alphabet agencies look more dangerous to me and my pocket book. Dec 11, 2014
- #CIA paid hush money to #Poland over secret prisons? I tell u they all are in it together most leaders in most countries. Dec 11, 2014
- Need a telephone number for #berkeleyprotests arrested can call to get legal and bail help. Twitter me and I will post. Dec 11, 2014

- #KobeBryant and other NBA stars join #ICantBreathe campaign. #BlackLivesMatter #berkeleyprotests #Ferguson Dec 11, 2014 🔗
- Is there one corporation in this country that is honest? Never mind. Silly question Dec 11, 2014 🔗
- @lacoguy u smarter than I am. Have to put on my cynical when dealing with these guys. Dec 11, 2014 🔗
- Protesters were leading in Time Magazine poll for "Person of the Year" Wonder what happened.? Dec 10, 2014 🔗
- #Reps trying to embed another giveaway to #wall street in 1.2t$ bill http://t.co/YLlo6j4eHG Dec 10, 2014 🔗
- Med-school students in five cities join "die-in protests #ICantBreathe protestors around the county, http://t.co/aVnbAtnKHk ... Dec 10, 2014 🔗
- #NYC quote: They can't arrest us all, can't kill us all, can they? No, but they sure want to scare us into thinking they might. Dec 10, 2014 🔗
- #NYC quote: Never underestimate the Freedom Dreams of Youth. You'll lose or sooner or later die anyway. Dec 10, 2014 🔗
- NYC quote: Its cold and wet out here but my feet are warm, head clear and I know this is the right place to be.#ICantBreathe #EricGarner Dec 10, 2014 🔗

- #NYC quote: These protesters look like the 60's. By-stander no, 60's kids had money, most of these kids, got no money no job. They'll stick Dec 10, 2014
- #Police Chief & officers join protester march with #BlackLivesMatter sign which went viral. photo & story at:http://t.co/XfLDsvsqZs Dec 10, 2014
- Police Chief in Richmond Ca. join protester march holding sign "#BlackLivesMatter which went viral. #berkeleyprotests Dec 10, 2014
- #Ferguson, #berkeleyprotests #BlackLivesMatter #ICantBreathe Protesters runner up in Time Magazine "Person of the Year" Award Dec 10, 2014
- Hard to believe but police friends are telling me that every demonstration like these have 10-30% police, feds, cia, fbi, out of towners. Dec 10, 2014
- Well this is my fight and it is a good one to fight. Goes all the way back to #Spartacus and beyond. Dec 10, 2014
- #NYC quote Can u be a beacon of democracy using cattle prods, broomsticks & water torture on people? Italy & Spain have warrants out, not us Dec 10, 2014
- Former Senator #Mark Udall speaks on the #CIATorture report. My view? Accountability starts at the top. See Udall at; http://t.co/KfUP7vltk2 Dec 10, 2014

- Sad, most of these kids never heard of #fascism. Comment on our educational system? Dec 10, 2014 🔗
- First rule of war and police action: "Destroy their will to resist." True u can look it up. Dec 10, 2014 🔗
- Better not to get arrested: jail, fines: best to demonstrate & be around to demonstrate again #berkeleyprotests Don't let'em surround u Dec 10, 2014 🔗
- @NYC quote: Don't know what they be thinking. We ain't no card board cutouts out here marching; real people front, left, right and back. Dec 10, 2014 🔗
- Stats show worldwide and historically that people after doing well and then forced suddenly back into poverty join uprisings. Dec 10, 2014 🔗
- 7.3 million people in jail, probation-parole. Most in the world 3 times over. #ICantBreathe #berkeleyprotests #EricGarner #Ferguson Dec 10, 2014 🔗
- 1/ 31 people in this country in jail or under probation-parole 7.3 million people! Most in the world 3 times over. http://t.co/cduvR3JRTr Dec 10, 2014 🔗
- Well my white friends tell me all the time: Nothing more terrifying than being forced back into poverty after having been middle class. True Dec 10, 2014 🔗

- Actually what I am saying that it is better not to get arrested: jail, fines, beatings: best to demonstrate & be around to demonstrate again Dec 10, 2014
- Cops and Highway patrol, #berkeleyprotests increasing bail arbitrarily on people. preying upon them, seizing their property, protesters say. Dec 10, 2014
- The protests in #Berkeley last night. At: https://t.co/6AFn8krxAw #Ferguson #ICantBreathe #BlackLivesMatter #EricGarner #HandsUpDontShoot Dec 10, 2014
- Sure I have an essay - book on race discrimination. #icantbreathe #ericgarner #berkeleyprotests #blacklivesmatter See http://t.co/gYoTRhQuQJ Dec 10, 2014
- Week of protests continues this week: today 37 cities. More later. Dec 10, 2014
- Refusing this black-white definition of who each of us are is key to future. Our skin color is the most important thing about us? Says who? Dec 10, 2014
- Well "white defining" started in slavery & has been maintained throughout our history culminating in GOP "Southern Strategy" still with us. Dec 10, 2014
- Political category meaning a short hand way of signaling who gets what when where and how: the very definition and purpose of politics. Dec 10, 2014

- What I mean is Italians English French Norwegians Germans all magically became "whites." How did that happen: why: who benefits who doesn't? Dec 10, 2014 ⚑
- The question is how did whites become white? "white" is a made up category to distinguish them from blacks. Totally a political category. Dec 10, 2014 ⚑
- #Hiliarious: made me laugh http://t.co/QLSWjz0wNV Dec 10, 2014 ⚑
- #US rejects cleanup of #nuclear sites as too "costly" http://t.co/Z5xrN0BTeP Dec 10, 2014 ⚑
- #FBI agents can pose as reporters? http://t.co/nn6zMDTqtk #Ferguson #BlackLivesMatter #berkeleyprotests #HandsUpDontShoot Dec 10, 2014 ⚑
- #Foxnews anchor Bill O'Reilly audience's median age? 72 yrs. 's plains a lot. #icantbreathe #berkeleyprotests http://t.co/X7XG3WEh0K Dec 10, 2014 ⚑
- http://t.co/CxMMOc5KXl #Ferguson #blacklivesmatter #Ferguson #ICantBreathe #EricGarner #NYC #HandsUpDontShoot #berkeleyprotests Dec 10, 2014 ⚑
- Need to know: Who or what is #ALEC ? #ICantBreathe ##ericgarner ##blacklivesmatter #berkeleyprotests #Ferguson #HandsUpWalkout Dec 10, 2014 ⚑

- Know the answers to all things. "I will or won't, it will or will not, true or false, yes - no, up-down, in between, so drop the worry bit. Dec 10, 2014
- Sage: U always felt different because u are. Now let's explore that. Dec 10, 2014
- This is an awesome piece of writing #icantbreathe #blacklivesmatter Confessions of (former) bad cop http://t.co/glfife34aw via @aNationRage Dec 10, 2014
- #Globalization a barbarity? #French right is left? http://t.co/U7357ZABzW Dec 10, 2014
- 2.5 million hits on Arizona cop chokehold #ICantBreathe http://t.co/EZZhW8qlvc Dec 10, 2014
- #McDonalds sales plummet. The Clown is Down. http://t.co/BPsL0fdAJ9 Dec 10, 2014
-
- Cop punches cuffed black woman walks free? #ICantBreathe #blacklivesmatter http://t.co/HJOV9RVwEg Dec 10, 2014
- Elites planning an escape to Mars? http://t.co/LU9eBw3CtS Dec 10, 2014
- NSA vs. ECU? http://t.co/f2ak9tLKqa Dec 10, 2014
- Germany acts like masters of the universe. Tensions in Europe. http://t.co/rYCnNtDW53 Dec 10, 2014

- The battle over austerity in Europe http://t.co/URQHomWHvx Dec 10, 2014 ⌐
- Privatizing cost britains 200lbs a month http://t.co/oChjRNkr2H Dec 10, 2014 ⌐
- More torture details at:http://t.co/XIFSYRfTiw Dec 09, 2014 ⌐
- #Chicago police blast "sweet home Alabama" in ghetto. #PoliceBrutality #ICantBreathe #BlackLivesMatter during…: http://t.co/o43Njhh5h6 Dec 09, 2014 ⌐
- Police shootings year by year, individual by individual 2009-2014 #ICantBreathe #BlackLivesMatter #EricGarner at:http://t.co/f2tapAb5ka Dec 09, 2014 ⌐
- Details of the torture used on detainees. http://t.co/XB72uP8yFf Dec 09, 2014 ⌐
- Even #CDC says current flu shot might not be a good match for this season flu strain. Really, then why recommend it? http://t.co/3yzsZUSrcc Dec 09, 2014 ⌐
- 40% of Americans don't trust flu shots. What does that tell you? #ICantBreathe #BlackLivesMatter #EricGarner http://t.co/c2OGmlali0 Dec 09, 2014 ⌐
- Torture report: Ugly ineffective torture procedures; world aghast, 60 bn $$ spent on

"security" zero real terrorism prevented or captured. Dec 09, 2014 ☞

- How a 49 year old mother of three ends up in jail on traffic violations.
  At: http://t.co/UiTKnyovVL ...#Ferguson #BlackLivesMatter Dec 09, 2014 ☞
- This year Santa has an awful lot of requests for bail and #ICantBreathe T-shirts Dec 09, 2014 ☞
- @NYC quote Honest to God, one cop joking to another cop, excuse me I'm going over to step on some necks. Dec 09, 2014 ☞
- The cops in Berkeley didn't understand that students at Berkeley do not expect to be batoned & hit in the head, parents got upset too. Dec 09, 2014 ☞
- You know that "consent of the governed" thing? Looks like they were just joshing us and putting us on. Dec 09, 2014 ☞
- What ever happened to governments deriving their powers from the consent of the governed? Ain't been no great lot of consenting lately. Dec 09, 2014 ☞
- Ok. R all whites bad? No, absolutely not. R all black people terrorists & rapists. No, absolutely not. Right fox news? So say so sometime. Dec 09, 2014 ☞
- No, MLK in the last year of his life was radical, anti-war, said riots often were the voice of the voiceless. One year later, he was killed. Dec 09, 2014 ☞

- #NYC quote: Foxnews: never heard of climate change; never heard of white elite privilege. Right #ICantBreathe #BlackLivesMatter Dec 09, 2014
- Totally unnecessary to arrest 150 in a peaceful demonstration. Why it occurs: leaders jailed, intimidate others. But million $$ lawsuits Dec 09, 2014
- Our Weekly Newspaper: #UnitedKingdom Edition #berkeleyprotests 12/18/14 Edition: #Ferguson, #democracynow #ICantBreathe Dec 09, 2014
- When u arrest 150: a sign of failure of the justice system. Mass arrests jam the jails beyond capacity, millions in law suits. Taxpayer pays Dec 09, 2014
- Hashtag #berkeleyprotests search results at: https://t.co/mKNQn1UUdq Dec 09, 2014
- Polls: majority of Americans disagree with the #EricGarner grand jury decision. #ICantBreathe #BlackLivesMatter #berkeleyprotests #Ferguson Dec 09, 2014
- @Rckayla the last two were. Police arrest people mainly to demoralize, get most vocal out of the way SOP Dec 09, 2014
- #berkeley third day of protests. 150 arrests. #berkeleyprotests #Ferguson #ICantBreathe At: http://t.co/0DBBedPvRV Dec 09, 2014
- The New Jim Crow: See below #ICantBreathe #BlackLivesMatter #EricGarner

#berkeleyprotests #HandsUpDontShoot #handsupwalkout #Ferguson Dec 09, 2014 ⌗

- Now u see how it all fits together. Why all the arrests, jail, warrants work toward the goal below: ... http://t.co/J2YNwbFyul Dec 09, 2014 ⌗

- In the era of colorblindness, it is no longer socially permissible to use race, explicitly, as a jus... http://t.co/5tYGnSvT2b Dec 09, 2014 ⌗

- #Sex #abuse among #Britons epidemic? http://t.co/eeAtIC43XJ Dec 09, 2014 ⌗

- One million #brits on food stamps. as Osborne ups austerity measures. http://t.co/IsSZKRcXY2 Dec 09, 2014 ⌗

- Bible: "Suffer to follow the children" "And the children to lead." Been that way in every society in the history of societies. Dec 09, 2014 ⌗

- Summing up. People Fed up. Dec 09, 2014 ⌗

- What sickens me is that the citizens of Ferguson will be taxed to pay for the new cop HQ "justice" department, and cop misconduct law suits. Dec 09, 2014 ⌗

- "Women of color are the fastest grown segment of the US prison population. What up with that?" Dec 09, 2014 ⌗

- DA's around this country regularly give immunity to cops who watched other cops kill. Why is that? Dec 09, 2014
- A badge is not a license to kill and tear gas is illegal to use in war but countries have made it legal to use on citizens. Why is that? Dec 09, 2014
- What to do? What the kids do. Expose the game. Tell congress this game ain't going to work. Dec 09, 2014
- @KateWalter12 thousands of people protest peaceful and media concentrations on a few violent types. Why? Dec 09, 2014
- Look. DA's are cops without uniforms. Dec 09, 2014
- DC cops protect protesters right to protest. Peaceful. Kudo's to DC police. Dec 09, 2014
- Every government in history conditions the population to see internal and external enemies, divide and rule, tax, squash resistance.That. Dec 09, 2014
- It's like we in America have been hypnotized to see things in black & white, oh no pun intended. Same thing happened in Germany. True that. Dec 09, 2014
- Most riots in this country are white riots wi/ the most property damage after basketball champion games, ditto football, college sports so Dec 09, 2014

- Every white serial killer is not representative of their race but every black protester is representative of their race. Duh? Dec 09, 2014 ⬚
- "If you have a good job, security and the like great, reach out and help somebody else who doesn't." Dec 09, 2014 ⬚
- Always enough money for suppression of citizens and war: Never enough money for jobs, schools, students, the poor, vets, poor whites, etc. Dec 09, 2014 ⬚
- #ICantBreathe hashtag search results https://t.co/rhEu4zaVoL Dec 09, 2014 ⬚
- A good protest movement creates new community, new friends, new support structures, marriages, lovers, fun, and alternatives to the cops. Dec 09, 2014 ⬚
- #berkeleyprotests #hashtag search results. at: https://t.co/6AFn8krxAw Dec 09, 2014 ⬚
- Can't happen here was heard last in Germany, in the soviet union in countless fascist states saying martial law was needed for 'security' Dec 09, 2014 ⬚
- If DA's in this country can indict a "ham sandwich" then I marching down to the local police station and passing out ham sandwich costumes. Dec 09, 2014 ⬚
- The larger point here is that it is not about blacks; it about an entire militarized police

army which can used against everybody. Germany? Dec 09, 2014

- Like I am fond of saying rather go this turmoil right now, than end up with the quiet that comes with resignation and a boot on the neck. Dec 09, 2014

- Key witness testimony in #Brown shooting: missing documents #Ferguson at: http://t.co/KJDtdVoAgo Dec 09, 2014

- The situation of young people in the US and around the world is getting worse and worse. At: http://t.co/9aFu9f3oc1 Dec 08, 2014

- That is a point: These police hit the streets treating American citizens like they are penned in #Palestinians? #BlackLivesMatter #Berkeley Dec 08, 2014

- Here is citation. Thought everyone knew about this. #ICantBreathe #BlackLivesMatter #berkeleyprotests See: https://t.co/HPqU96aqWi Dec 08, 2014

- True. Police in last 10 years get free trips to Israel for "terrorists" training and now we see them using it on the streets against kids. Dec 08, 2014

- Well, for last time, a crowd trapped will tend to get peeved and try to bust out. Dec 08, 2014

- The old days cops-protesters would agree on a route and/or agreed upon assembly area. No problem 2nd night 'cause agreement & common sense. Dec 08, 2014

- Yes, I know Berkeley, TV never shows crowd surrounded, penned. Move, disperse to where? First rule of demonstration: don't let'm surround u. Dec 08, 2014 ⚑
- Berkeley? Old tactics, surround crowd, yell move or disperse meantime at other end of street prevent them from dispersing. Trap beat arrest. Dec 08, 2014 ⚑
- Don't have to be super smart to know when you are in the middle of a growing holocaust. Dec 08, 2014 ⚑
- Why Oakland erupts all the time See this map. At:http://t.co/YjvkHVVuQc #ICantBreathe #BlackLivesMatter #HandsUpDontShoot #berkeleyprotests Dec 08, 2014 ⚑
- Well I think as long as cops keep shooting & harassing anyone: blacks, whites, youth, students, it'll fuel more turmoil. 500 a yr. killed?!! Dec 08, 2014 ⚑
- Advertisers focus on kids 'cause they spend 40b a year but nag parents for stuff they see on TV, Cell phones= 740b. yr Advertisers know this Dec 08, 2014 ⚑
- "Moment u let your kids plop down in front of TV, cell phones: anywhere advertisers can get to them, u have lost them to the corporate ghouls Dec 08, 2014 ⚑
- "War is consumable product sold to kids early on when they don't know any better." Dec 08, 2014 ⚑

- "Any country that makes life cheap in overseas wars, sooner or later will make life cheap at home." Dec 08, 2014
- True, maybe if we had protests "by invitation only" we could keep the uninvited out. Dec 08, 2014
- In Washington DC lawmakers have implemented their "Hide behind the holidays, so we don't have to do or say anything about protests" Strategy Dec 08, 2014
- March: Washington this Saturday 12/13/14. #ICantBreathe #Ferguson #BlackLivesMatter #HandsUpDontShoot #HandsUpWalkout http://t.co/iiY6NLxKPv Dec 08, 2014
- Did #Hitler live, escape to Argentina and die in1962 rich? #video #naziwatch Dec 08, 2014
- Scary if true:: Most of the Nazi leaders were within the normal psychological range, not psychopaths, ordinary people. Tested after the war. Dec 08, 2014
- Am I paranoid? Humm, warming up to it. Even paranoids have real enemies. Dec 08, 2014
- #NYC quote: U got a gun, teargas, taser, tanks, rubber bullets, blue gangs, & u telling me all u have to do is claim fear & u can shoot me? Dec 08, 2014

- "The price of freedom is eternal vigilance" Somebody said that. It rings true. Dec 08, 2014 ⎙
- Well, just saying, walk through the halls of congress & yell out "sociopath" they all raise their hands up.#handsupcongress (humor, I think) Dec 08, 2014 ⎙
- @Desertsaffron @George_Osborne True. When u yell out sociopaths-they all raise their hands. Dec 08, 2014 ⎙
- #NYC quote: Why don't I ever see this headline? "Cops Riot: Beat and Arrest Protesters. #Ferguson #berkeleyprotests #ICantBreathe Dec 08, 2014 ⎙
- There's a whole permanent underclass: women, students, poor, vets, immigrants, browns, blacks that will be protesting until change happens. Dec 08, 2014 ⎙
- #NYC quote: This is a white rage white supremacy counter revolution after civil rights gains of 60's. Dec 08, 2014 ⎙
- 2nd night of protests #berkeleyprotests #oakland http://t.co/6D77w01MCX Dec 08, 2014 ⎙
- NFL players show support for #EricGarner http://t.co/n6ohVTjWMK Dec 08, 2014 ⎙
- #Austerity in #uk. Osborne doubles down http://t.co/Whjs4GU96f Dec 08, 2014 ⎙

- #NYC quote: These grand juries split legal hairs to free cops and ignore cops out here splitting heads. Dec 08, 2014
- cops acquitted in attack on black female #blacklivesmatter #HandsUpDontShoot #ICantBreathe http://t.co/T3537ZvTMP Dec 08, 2014
- Another chokehold video: Arizonia. #icantbreathe #ericgarner http://t.co/QmfgN1OFXw Dec 08, 2014
- #justice department: #police investigations what is the record? http://t.co/w89imAXgKU Dec 08, 2014
- #berkeleyprotests #Berkeley http://t.co/B1ALXcMb7n Dec 08, 2014
- The week in photos: #icantbreathe #blacklivesmatter #Ferguson #HandsUpDontShoot #HandsUpWalkout #EricGarner Dec 08, 2014
- Our weekly newspaper is out 12-7-14 Edition. #Ferguson #ICantBreathe #HandsUpWalkout #BlackLivesMatter #berkeleyprotests #HandsUpDontShoot Dec 08, 2014
- How u gonna make it through the day without, art, love, sex, music, politics, community, family, poetry, writing, reading,? Answer me that. Dec 08, 2014

- Sex? I am for it. Here is an essay how and why. "The Body O"
  At: http://t.co/PppYimbupl Dec 08, 2014 &
- Chicago pastors led protest. #Ferguson #BlackLivesMatter
  #ICantBreathe http://t.co/kxjP34Mcl2 Dec 08, 2014 &
- Spirituality is not airy-fairy bunk. It is your next level of advancement dude. Dec 08, 2014 &
- I am not raising hell I am raising spiritual connections between those previously unconnected. Yes that is subversive. So be it. Dec 08, 2014 &
- IMHO u cannot be a great leader if you have slaughtered, plundered the lives of the people you end up ruling. History bks try to sell u that Dec 08, 2014 &
- True that sir #bullying early in life preps the young for domination by the strong.
  At: http://t.co/6XwpMqn1sa Dec 08, 2014 &
- #History of #freedom vs. #domination? Yes. here is a #book-#essay on this
  at: http://t.co/1nlmgWNRda & part 2 http://t.co/KFfjdh9M7p Dec 08, 2014 &
- The history of every society on this planet is the history of the constant battle between the forces of domination & the forces of freedom. Dec 08, 2014 &
- No. Jesus was a great man: C essays & novels I have written

at: http://t.co/HuglysvICI & http://t.co/10kmIWgd 5P &http://t.co/AxdbOGO9kA Dec 08, 2014 ⇗

- Don't have to be super smart: have a lot of money, to know the difference between right and wrong. Dec 08, 2014 ⇗
- Well u can go through life, head down neck ready for the guillotine, or you can look around to unite with others and escape that fate. Dec 08, 2014 ⇗
- Jesus washed the feet of the poor, didn't like the super-rich, was a communalist, scourged by the Romans, is still remembered. Duh. Dec 08, 2014 ⇗
- You can't kill an idea whose time has come, but man, there are folks in every society who sure like trying. Dec 08, 2014 ⇗
- When you hate, you are already dead. Dec 08, 2014 ⇗
- Beauty is the brave, engaged, smart, committed person, who acts on noble beliefs & loves more than just himself, herself or their own. Dec 08, 2014 ⇗
- You are young forever if you believe in something. You are old if you believe in nothing but u and yours then u slowly wither. Dec 08, 2014 ⇗
- How old am I? Old enough not to fall for the same power games they have used for decades. Out them, shame them, jail the jailers. Dec 08, 2014 ⇗

- Entrenched power hates everyone who cannot give power more power. Dec 08, 2014
- When one went down in front of the line, two more took their place. Dec 08, 2014
- In the sixties, women in teargas white, showed up & put stringed flowers on the national guard bayonets. The visual in the end stopped a war Dec 08, 2014
- Seen too much violence to be violent, seen too much love to embrace hate, been too educated to fall for propaganda. Dec 08, 2014
- I was, in my youth, raised on teargas, radicalized by knowledge, educated by real people, and became clear-eyed by head-bashing. Dec 08, 2014
- Most of what they do is for "shock and awe" intimidate you from showing up for free speech, then gas'em, tank'em arrest leaders. Scare"em. Dec 08, 2014
- Hardest thing to understand in this America, people in power don't like u, want to see u fail and will do violence on u. Way it is. Dec 08, 2014
- Book: Yes I plan a book. If u haven't figured this out yet this is history playing out on the streets.. I'm documenting it day by day. Dec 08, 2014
- Scariest thing for elites: people out there with their strollers & kids. To them it means

mainstream support. They go crazy. Round 1 to folks Dec 08, 2014

- Closer a movement comes to becoming mainstream more the propaganda machine will attempt to discredit it.."violent" rift-raft, "crazies, etc. Dec 08, 2014

- Why would cops & national guard stay by & do nothing? They have an interest in discrediting any mass movement. More overtime, TV, budgets. Dec 07, 2014

- #Ferguson, #NYC #OccupyWallStreet all had people assigned to stopping violence. Hard to control if cops are standing by & letting it happen. Dec 07, 2014

- The danger of any movement is not allowing it to be hijacked by people with other agendas, violent cops, provocateurs, violent types etc. Dec 07, 2014

- Well whatever the sign says I know most people are doing "civil disobedience" & that means resisting peacefully unjust laws. Dec 07, 2014

- @bootsiecali Sorry civil disobedience is resisting and it is not violent. True you don't want to be labeled "subversive" . Dec 07, 2014

- #NeoNazi 's making gains in Europe? That is trouble. See at: http://t.co/nS99OHoU6l Dec 07, 2014

- Protests morphing into a resistance movement? Some say so. #Ferguson #ICantBreathe #EricGarner #BlackLivesMatter At: http://t.co/Mk308pc1OP Dec 07, 2014
- Right and Left United on the #EricGarner case? Because of this unity a movement has momentum. We shall see. http://t.co/HhsOWqQzZ4 Dec 07, 2014
- Political songs: "Welcome to the Machine", Pink Floyd; "Boulevard of Broken Dreams", Green Day; "The Torture Never Stops", Frank Zappa. Dec 07, 2014
- Hell if they are going to spy on my life 24-7 I am going to text and suggest lunch on them & save time by giving up all my info at 1 time. Dec 07, 2014
- NSA can spy on 70% of cell phones? Means I have to really get my selfie together. My nose looks more like a snout. http://t.co/1aPJA4dnUZ Dec 07, 2014
- NSA can spy on 70% of the world's cell phones? Does that mean I can text them to send out for pizza for me. Why not? Dec 07, 2014
- Anarchists high-jack peaceful protest? CBS news at: http://t.co/SEnKRcG0dK #berkeleyprotests Dec 07, 2014
- #berkeleyprotests #Berkeley erupts. More info. At: http://t.co/ZYPpgrDtTU Dec 07, 2014

- Wal-Mart? More like "Push US Up Against The Wal-Mart. Dec 07, 2014 ⊕
- Hey u are right those song titles work just as well as a description of many of our love lives. Dec 07, 2014 ⊕
- Sure if you have some titles tweet them directly, or send to me and I will post. Dec 07, 2014 ⊕
- The American political system in song titles: "Can't get me no satisfaction" "U ruined me" "Ball and Chain" Joplin "What's Going On" M.Gaye " Dec 07, 2014 ⊕
- Hey, let's hear it for our elephant sisters and bros. Dec 07, 2014 ⊕
- Did mention that elephants are a matriarchal society, never forget, ferociously protect their young and open carry two sharp tusks.? Yeah. Dec 07, 2014 ⊕
- I like elephants. The only animal in the jungle that goes Lion-Swatting. Dec 07, 2014 ⊕
- Too much? Ok. Here is another possibility from #KirkFranklin " I Smile" Beautiful video. Amazing At: https://t.co/waw37SV3OP Dec 07, 2014 ⊕
- Every movement needs an anthem or song. My choice: Spiritual Rock @kirkfranklin #BlackLivesMatter "Revolution" At: https://t.co/zcs7TX3Paf Dec 07, 2014 ⊕

- Elephants are on strike at the zoos? Apparently they, like many of us, they are tired of working for peanuts. Dec 07, 2014 🖻
- Well what I hear: "Tanks out." Police Army out of our lives. No jail fines warrants killings and beatings. That. Dec 07, 2014 🖻
- Just noting in Mexico 43 students killed. They have been protesting for weeks: growing not giving up. Government may fall. Dec 07, 2014 🖻
- More protests expected across nation. This time correct article I hope. http://t.co/2qPKEfAb56 Dec 07, 2014 🖻
- Over 21 cities have made it illegal to feed the homeless right along with the pigeons & zoo animals? Dec 07, 2014 🖻
- My point: if u never hear a point of view different than yr own u gain the illusion u are right about everything. Not. Dec 07, 2014 🖻
- #NYC quote: Truth to power: They incompetent - don't care or evil. Most likely all three. #Ferguson #blacklivesmatter #handsupwalkout Dec 07, 2014 🖻
- Well my point is that more crimes are embedded in racist, class-based laws than anywhere else. #Ferguson #blacklivesmatter Dec 07, 2014 🖻
- #NYC: The "loosie" strategy: criminalize everything - excuse to confront blacks. Drive

'em out: jail'em: Shoot'em. #icantbreathe Dec 07, 2014 ⟐

- The stupidity is a few rioting cops r creating a generation of radicals with tanks & teargas. America doing same abroad. Is this a plan? Dec 07, 2014 ⟐
- This is becoming "kiss my ring" "hands up" "get down on the ground" "knee in the neck" America? Dec 07, 2014 ⟐
- True. Cops kill more per year than died in a year in Iraq. We had/have a war abroad and also 1 back home on blacks. #blacklivesmatter Dec 07, 2014 ⟐
- Black churches holler back "can I get witness?" Now with police that is a serious question. Dec 07, 2014 ⟐
- Whites expose police racial bias #Ferguson #HandsUpDontShoot #blacklivesmatter #handsupwalkout #crimingwhilewhite http://t.co/1ilvaFsevY Dec 07, 2014 ⟐
- Why? If a criminal gang was shooting dead 500 people a year we'd declare a national emergency. Cops? We do nothing. #Ferguson Dec 07, 2014 ⟐
- #Ferguson Obama administration to continue racial profiling at airports. #berkeley #Ican'tbreathe #handsupwalkout http://t.co/SZDCNSgs2h Dec 07, 2014 ⟐

- #nazi toys for holiday season? message here? #ICantBreathe #HandsUpDontShoot #berkeley #HandsUpWalkout http://t.co/hRJvpCBPAU Dec 07, 2014 🔗
- #Athens erupts #berkekey #icantbreathe #EricGarner http://t.co/OGCTAWK1Uo Dec 07, 2014 🔗
- #Berkeley is in the house. #Ferguson #blacklivesmatter #handsupwalkout http://t.co/4Lf60doG9Y Dec 07, 2014 🔗
- Women, blacks, poor, vets, immigrants, browns, the young. Why are we warring on these people they don't have any oil. #Ferguson Dec 07, 2014 🔗
- More on the Wisconsin case background. "Ferguson at: http://t.co/jueggCIQYq Dec 07, 2014 🔗
- Here story on the Wisconsin Police Custody Law. At: http://t.co/oFVDRFbVj3 #Ferguson Dec 07, 2014 🔗
- My tombstone: I thinking about something like: Born (insert year) Insert dash Died (insert year) Then it should say "really worked that dash Dec 06, 2014 🔗
- My grandmothers last dying words. "Don't have time for dying. Too much to do. Ok maybe just this one time." She was a funny lady. Dec 06, 2014 🔗

- "If u don't have a seat at the table,you're probably on the menu..word" Don't know who said it but I'm checking to see if I have name plate Dec 06, 2014 ⊡
- Wisconsin 1st state to require independent investigation of people who are harmed or die in police custody. 49 more states to go. #Ferguson Dec 06, 2014 ⊡
- I am saying: that If our politicians were in my Democracy class, I would flunk the lot. Dec 06, 2014 ⊡
- 4,491 U.S. service members killed in Iraq between 2003 and 2014. Justifiable homicide killings=400 per year. Tot. 2003-14=4,400 #icantbreathe Dec 06, 2014 ⊡
- Don't miss any #Tweets. See them all #Ferguson, #HandsUpWalkout at: http://t.co/0NQCLhcy89 ... press "get tweets" to see them. Dec 06, 2014 ⊡
- If u see dead babies in the river, u can develop a rescue program or u can say hell I am going up river to c who is throwing them in. Dec 06, 2014 ⊡
- "I hear u are sick of the turmoil. Not me. I prefer this turmoil to the quiet which a boot on the neck will bring." Dec 06, 2014 ⊡
- College kids and professional sports people starting to get involved. at; http://t.co/56v5j6UR85 Dec 06, 2014 ⊡

- Elites? I mean millionaire politicians, media moguls, dumpy generals, billionaires, wall street, spy agencies, all of whom talk to each other Dec 06, 2014 ⚐
- Don't know. Feels like have to hit elites in this country in the wallet. That is where their hearts are located. Dec 06, 2014 ⚐
- Nothing scares world elites more than hundreds-thousands of young people, determined, cross racial, cross-continents zeroing in on the truth Dec 06, 2014 ⚐
- #NYC Worldwide protests & where are our leaders? Bickering over how much to take away from the poor & give to the rich. #BlackLivesMatter Dec 06, 2014 ⚐
- @GardenerMiss Yep. Apparently taught to NYPD by Israeli consultants Dec 06, 2014 ⚐
- They used military tactics on us: isolate & pen'em into small groups, surround them, yell disperse, making sure they can't, &then arrest "em Dec 06, 2014 ⚐
- @NYC What I see out here is not only suppression but a damned ugly glee about applying it by some of these cops. #Ferguson #BlackLivesMatter Dec 06, 2014 ⚐
- IF YOU HAVE BEEN ARRESTED AT A DEMONSTRATION, PLEASE CONTACT THE NLG-NYC HOTLINE AT 212-679-6018 #ShutItDown #ICantBreathe Dec 06, 2014 ⚐

- #NYC The stupidest thing in the world was to create a permanent underclass of students, blacks, women, prisoners, vets, & the poor. Trouble. Dec 06, 2014 ⚐
- #NYC quote: If they listen closely they will hear the sound of a lot of feet on the ground, on the move. Can't kill us all. #Ferguson Dec 06, 2014 ⚐
- 40 million Google Hits on #Ferguson #ICantBreathe #BlackLivesMatter #HandsUpDontShoot at: https://t.co/Vxi0TGhbSm Dec 06, 2014 ⚐
- Protests #EricGarner #Ferguson spread worldwide. #SanFrancisco, #NYC #TOKYO4FERGUSON . London at: http://t.co/Mk308pc1OP Dec 06, 2014 ⚐
- #NYC quote: the real grand jury verdict is being voted on in the streets. Happens when the system is crooked. #BlackLivesMatter #EricGarner Dec 06, 2014 ⚐
- #NYC quote: Too many deaths, too many funerals, too many excuses, no accountability #BlackLivesMatter #ICantBreathe #HandsUpDontShoot . Dec 06, 2014 ⚐
- Shooting unarmed black man in a stairwell by NYPD sparks new protests. #ICantBreathe #BlackLivesMatter #Ferguson At: http://t.co/CcBghdmi0o Dec 06, 2014 ⚐
- U might be right. Maybe there is a decades long war on blacks, browns, women, in this

country. Multiple institutions involved. #ICantBreathe Dec 06, 2014 

- #NYC cop: Blacks apply to be a cop. They are told u have "heart murmur" women told "scoliosis"-disqualified. Exam doctors-whole system rotten Dec 06, 2014 

- #NYC quote: We know police informants: always super militant: provoke cops. Get arrested with u but separated in the tank from us-released Dec 06, 2014 

- #NYC quote: They keep telling us they against mob rule. Hell what they think. They already have organized mob rule. That's why we marching. Dec 06, 2014 

- #NYC #akai gurley #December 6 actions planned for today. #unarmed black man Gurley was the stairwell killing by nypd cop #ICantBreathe Dec 06, 2014 

- #NYC quote: This movement went international when Darren Wilson in a paid national interview said he would kill "demon" MichaelBrown again. Dec 06, 2014 

- #Ferguson happened because of white rage? What is white rage? #ICantBreathe #HandsUpDontShoot #EricGarner http://t.co/J74UIJ9fCI Dec 06, 2014 

- #Ferguson.what the foreign #press is saying http://t.co/qUvdKKEZIz Dec 06, 2014

- #Ferguson & outside agitators http://t.co/vlPnCyzkVG Dec 06, 2014
- Protesters likely time magazine's "Person of the Year" #Ican'tbreathe #Ferguson #HandsUpDontShoot #blacklivesmatter Dec 06, 2014
- Takes a lot of commitment to get out in the cold wet streets every day for a black kid u didn't even know. I applaud them. These r our youth Dec 06, 2014
- Here is article to go with chart below #Ferguson disparity in arrests exists nationwide. See at: http://t.co/EAWGMrtMCh Dec 06, 2014
- Does your county have a greater disparity of racial arrests than #Ferguson? See your state and your county at: http://t.co/9cV5ipmORv ... Dec 06, 2014
- #Ericgarner protests clog six major cities at; http://t.co/SOm61E7S42 #BlackLivesMatter #HandsUpDontShoot Dec 06, 2014
- "He/she that is not growing every day is busy dying" paraphrasing #BobDylan Dec 06, 2014
- #Mozart the Movie three parts. Gotta see this at:#music at: https://t.co/prX1vvJ8ZL Dec 06, 2014
- #MichaelJackson "Smile" at:https://t.co/4C54toYT33 Dec 06, 2014

- "So my generation is confused: U make it sound like a bad thing. We confused are the only answer." Dec 06, 2014 🔗
- #music don't know what this song is about. But I know soul when I see it. https://t.co/mHb9qAxb8u Dec 06, 2014 🔗
- "Don't know what u don't know. Can't imagine if u haven't taken the time to dream, can't act to help if you don't taken the time to love." Dec 06, 2014 🔗
- If u have a problem but no idea of a solution, stick around. If u have a problem & think there is only 1 answer, leave. If u are not sure ok Dec 06, 2014 🔗
- "A liberal is 1 who hasn't been mugged, a conservative's one who has, a radical is 1 who the cops mugged. #HandsUpWalkout #HandsUpDontShoot Dec 06, 2014 🔗
- #NYC Quote "Why should I let some fat military bureaucrat tell me who I should kill?" Dec 06, 2014 🔗
- It's not just about the police: it's about a generation fed up; about power pitting us against 1 another, it's about our future, not theirs. Dec 06, 2014 🔗
- Excuse me: If you grab my body & choke my neck over a loosie, something here is very wrong. #icantbreathe, #Ferguson, #HandsUpDontShoot shoot Dec 06, 2014 🔗
- Do I sleep? Not if they don't. Dec 06, 2014 🔗

- What I mean if u haven't been arrested and given the "u a minority treatment" you don't know whereof u speak. Dec 06, 2014
- "The capacity to feel joy for the happiness of the other is what it means to be human." Dec 06, 2014
- So It's becoming "kiss my ring" "Shut Up" "Get Down or u get arrested: America? #ICantBreathe #HandsUpDontShoot ##BlackLivesMatter Dec 06, 2014
- #MariahCarey #music "We Belong Together" https://t.co/zyTeuwCo0k Dec 06, 2014
- "Hardest thing for the young to learn: Everything today is not forever. Hardest thing for the old to understand: Tomorrow is only tomorrow." Dec 06, 2014
- #Music "Bruce Hornsby at https://t.co/WtpU7IRB5P Dec 06, 2014
- #Music #batsforlashes "All your Gold" at: https://t.co/U1ujJvUA5Q Dec 06, 2014
- #BobMarley "Turn your lights down low Feat. #LaurenHill at: https://t.co/WzxY9so2hK Dec 06, 2014
- #Music Timothy Bloom "Till The End of Time" https://t.co/8Qt9aCkYat ...#HandsUpDo ntShoot #BlackLivesMatter #EricGarner #Ferguson Dec 06, 2014
- #Music "Silver Springs" #Fleetwood Mac https://t.co/HgLhdjlsSA Dec 06, 2014

- # Music "Revolution" #kirk Franklin #HandsUpDontShoot #handsup #HandsUpWalkout #Ferguson #BlackLivesMatter https://t.co/zcs7TX3Paf Dec 06, 2014
- #music #Rihanna "stay" https://t.co/okbLgrwHMK Dec 06, 2014
- #music black light "one call" https://t.co/OJ4TAap3aq Dec 06, 2014
- #music the veronicas :"u ruined me" https://t.co/kGG8qg1nCi Dec 06, 2014
- my #music funny valentine https://t.co/dVkb1reK7T Dec 06, 2014
- black man shot by white cop in Phoenix autopsy maneuvers at #icantbreathe http://t.co/ec08ut4eRq Dec 06, 2014
- #NYC #icantbreate #BlackLivesMatter third night of protest at: http://t.co/YzTzxpzQTN Dec 06, 2014
- Choke hold cop: Not his first rodeo. other claims https://t.co/FIfgURgLWx #EricGarner #HandsUpDontShoot #HandsUpWalkout #BlackLivesMatter Dec 06, 2014
- Memory is the great reservoir of our lives. Be sure it is filled at all times. Dec 06, 2014
- Touch my scones, my latte and u die. Dec 06, 2014

- Nothing more sexy, endearing, and adorable, than a person that does not know that they are sexy, endearing and adorable. Dec 06, 2014 &
- I used to be smart but damn I started to think I was smart. Dec 06, 2014 &
- Never be a defendant for what u believe or feel: nor a judge of what others feel, think and hope for. U ain't that smart or transcended. Dec 06, 2014 &
- Never offer advice, unless asked, and never before you have learned to shut up and listen. Dec 06, 2014 &
- Education these days is the slow process of understanding what does not make sense in terms of what they were telling u.. Science included. Dec 06, 2014 &
- Heads talk, minds explain, spirits commune. Love merges. Souls transcend. Dec 06, 2014 &
- If u see dead babies in the river, u can develop a rescue program or u can say hell I am going up river to c who is throwing them in. Dec 06, 2014 &
- @downriver_b can never have too much law and order, but never anything about what is causing the problem? Dec 06, 2014 &
- Hell why do people like vampire movies and TV shows? Because somewhere deep down they know somebody IS sucking their blood. & they r right Dec 06, 2014 &

- A zombie-fied mind seldom knows it has been zombefied. Dec 06, 2014 ⏍
- @downriver_b U are so correct. Longest running TV show in history. That is no accident. Want keep the message in front of the zombies. Dec 06, 2014 ⏍
- De-educate 'em from age 2, teach'em wrong history, weed out the rebels, punish & jail the poor & the rebels, give money to the whites. USA. Dec 06, 2014 ⏍
- It's like if you don't really have an opinion u have really looked into there is all these media people happy to give u one. Brain zombie. Dec 06, 2014 ⏍
- Don't seem complicated tome: Cops keep the tanks in the armory, respect protesters, No cop riot. No problem.#ICantBreathe #HandsUpDontShoot Dec 06, 2014 ⏍
- Can't watch even news shows with propaganda muck messing up my evening. Dec 06, 2014 ⏍
- @seminole2419 Yeah. That's right. Most of these generals are from the pentagon Dec 06, 2014 ⏍
- I get tweets from people who lecture me about black communities who have never lived in a black community. What up? Dec 06, 2014 ⏍
- Just because you get taller and make money, don't make you smarter about other people you

- have no continuing experience with. Dec 06, 2014
- Let's get this one straight. Most of the billion dollar media industry, NBC, CBS, NPR, Foxnews, movies, all of it is pure propaganda. Dec 05, 2014
- Let's get this straight middle class, white & poor people, whites and most blacks don't riot. Period. So who does. Let's investigate that. Dec 05, 2014
- Every pundit TV show ought to have a banner below each pundit which states where the get their income from, like political commercials. Dec 05, 2014
- Don't seem complicated to me: Cops keep the tanks in the armory, respect protesters, No cop riot. No problems. Dec 05, 2014
- She: As a teenager nobody got me He: I'm willing to get u That would be just swell She: Get over here He U can get me too. She 2 gets =a got Dec 05, 2014
- It's not that nobody likes me it's that I have not taken the time to like them yet. Too much work. Dec 05, 2014
- He said: "What u looking at?" She said "Nothing" He: "Quick wit that's what I love about u. He: My love is all about u. She: c'mon over here Dec 05, 2014

- 140 poetry: "Nobody likes me now I have them where they want me. I'm apparently inscrutable" Dec 05, 2014 ⮑
- 140 poetry: I have moments gleaming in twilight's quickened gloaming you glide into that sacred space in the hearts space's lilting memory Dec 05, 2014 ⮑
- "Funny on the Web" "As a boy I so unattractive, I could stand on the railroad tracks and get a freight train to take the dirt road." Dec 05, 2014 ⮑
- No it is not I don't like classical music. Just particular. Here are my selections: http://t.co/DjiCStWni5 Dec 05, 2014 ⮑
- 10 most crime ridden states? Mostly rural states, not big city states, mostly white pop. states, mostly gun states. http://t.co/X9sSiTYQyA .. Dec 05, 2014 ⮑
- #Police jobs safer than many other jobs. They are not even in the top ten. Job is getting more safe not less See: http://t.co/W3NrCyEBog Dec 05, 2014 ⮑
- @Future_of_West Here is one link. http://t.co/LYoVqB2y0x They have racial data too. FBI Dec 05, 2014 ⮑
- No, no crime rates have been dropping for years, but police budgets way up. Why is that? Dec 05, 2014 ⮑

- Cops are in black hoods cause cops, judges, DA's all depend upon the fines, arrests and jailing of blacks for their salaries. Dec 05, 2014

- Most crimes: committed by whites so why are the cops so much in black hoods? Dec 05, 2014

- The fact: most crimes are committed by whites- against other whites, in non-urban states, white gun states. Blacks crime on blacks but fewer Dec 05, 2014

- The racist undertone cops encourage is "If I wasn't here, the "urban" element would rape, rob & loot. I am the finger in the dam. Balderdash Dec 05, 2014

- @mzacharyjohnson Humm, u have a point. I relent. It just that classical music does not respect the young & their music. A big mistake. Dec 05, 2014

- I am saying cops don't want to be scrutinized or held accountable in how they do their jobs, get another job. Dec 05, 2014

- @omamaine Right, Called Choke-hold a "model" cop. That union needs to be brought down, not innocent citizens. Dec 05, 2014

- I saying that a country that doesn't respect its women is not a country, it is a big male frat house , or worse. Real men respect women. Dec 05, 2014

- 1/2 the women in this country: been sexually assaulted, groped, raped: Many get verbally assaulted walking down the street. This is good? Dec 05, 2014 ⚐
- Fact: SOME cops assault, rape, batter & extort sex from women, especially prostitutes, steal or plant drugs. Should not be protecting them. Dec 05, 2014 ⚐
- Want? People want cops, tanks, tear gas & the rest out of their everyday lives. Tank the tanks, pull the troops back. get some real officers Dec 05, 2014 ⚐
- @mzacharyjohnson Sir maybe I overstated my case a bit. But neurotic is highly emotional, & cold is lack of empathy. peasant music is dissed. Dec 05, 2014 ⚐
- #NYC quote: "Being a cop is like being in a gang, can't snitch on a brother, if you do you could get hurt." Dec 05, 2014 ⚐
- Take courage: put yr hand out to those you disagree with, that is called peace. Takes same courage to accept that hand. Those 4 war hate this Dec 05, 2014 ⚐
- Being 4 unity does not mean u become wishy-washy. It means u are joining with others to overcome those who benefit from & perpetuate division Dec 05, 2014 ⚐
- @frankie0914 Not what I am reading. You got the right hash? U don't get it. Getting out of a

ticket big deal for POCs It goes to warrant Dec 05, 2014

- Right. Thanks to all people of good will who have spoken out about #EricGarner blacks, whites, old, young, even officers from everywhere. Tx Dec 05, 2014
- In #NYC an EMT, a Nurse, a Doctor police must report abuse by police of those in custody. Does it happen? Not. ##ICantBreathe Dec 05, 2014
- Remember the British forces forced colonists to put up troops in their houses! To feed them, tea not the problem: troops were the problem. Dec 05, 2014
- It is clear to me there's a big difference between a police force & an occupying army. A revolution started in this country over just this. Dec 05, 2014
- #CrimingWhileWhite Whites confess different treatment for them by cops. Dec 05, 2014
- @KathyAngel2 Good point. Let's see how it plays out. Fluid situation. Dec 05, 2014
- @GlorifieDGoD Could be. Could be. DA here does not just hand out immunity. Had that battle. Plea bargain yes, immunity no. Dec 05, 2014
- @KathyAngel2 I am. Some can stay, but got to move to next steps. The lesson of occupy. Need an outcome not just marching. Dec 05, 2014

- @LisaDix41219475 You are funny! Good to know. Dec 05, 2014 ⌕
- @LisaDix41219475 U breaking up with me? (smile) I broke up with you first. (smile) Dec 05, 2014 ⌕
- @KathyAngel2 Amen.They do that in Wisconsin of places.Would go a long way toward quieting the streets, & restore some confidence before 2016 Dec 05, 2014 ⌕
- @LisaDix41219475 Nope. Just people that I follow. And besides after a while best to agree to disagree right? Dec 05, 2014 ⌕
- @LisaDix41219475 Come on Lisa. Smile. It's only a difference of opinion. We are both good people Right? Dec 05, 2014 ⌕
- @KathyAngel2 Wish I had that kind of faith. Justice department is still "investigating" the #Trayvon case. Dec 05, 2014 ⌕
- @LisaDix41219475 You just love talking to me. Muslim countries. No, I live here and I want to fix it where I live. Lisa, lets break up. :) Dec 05, 2014 ⌕
- @GlorifieDGoD Good try. I have lots of black cop friends. They are there because they feel better them than one of the citizen killers Dec 05, 2014 ⌕
- @LisaDix41219475 Does this apply to cops too? If u really think so, write a letter or something. Dec 05, 2014 ⌕

- @KathyAngel2 Now why would he do that? Bet you a burrito, they don't get indicted. who's left to indict after all these maneuvers? No one. Dec 05, 2014 ⚐
- Upholding the law should apply to everyone. Dec 05, 2014 ⚐
- @GlorifieDGoD Well, some quit. Corruption is corruption. I would quit. Dec 05, 2014 ⚐
- Ok, But the 4 other cops who stood around and did nothing about an banned chokehold ought to be indicted. Doing nothing is a felony 4 a cop. Dec 05, 2014 ⚐
- @GlorifieDGoD I get that. But in court they can tell the truth about police procedures, what they have seen on force--and they never do. Dec 05, 2014 ⚐
- @GlorifieDGoD Sure they do all the time. See the "cop page" Ferguson police. had KKK references and everything. Public Dec 05, 2014 ⚐
- @GlorifieDGoD Sure wish the media, sixty minutes or so would put one of them up to describe what it is like behind the "The Big Blue Wall" Dec 05, 2014 ⚐
- @GlorifieDGoD Really. Cop out. No pun intended. And self-serving too. They can speak off the record if they wanted to. Dec 05, 2014 ⚐
- Where do we get idea of "cop as hero?" Killing kids, sneak choke-holds, killing unarmed

people is not bravery, it is cowardice. Afraid? Quit Dec 05, 2014 ⬚

- Twitter me your signs and I will post on twitter the good ones. @Lnnie Dec 05, 2014 ⬚
- Out of 5,000 cops in #NYC has a single one spoke out against #ericgarner? Most afraid of retaliation if they do. Somebody ought to ask 'em Dec 05, 2014 ⬚
- Tweet below: They all participate in this: their jobs depend upon blacks, & guess what; blacks pay taxes to support their own oppression. Dec 05, 2014 ⬚
- Stepping back it's not just an occupying police army, they are supported by occupying institutions: courts, hospitals, slum lords, all in it Dec 05, 2014 ⬚
- #EricGarner case not just cops, it's the EMT's, the nurses, the doctors, the DA's, the public defenders, the judges, all participate in this. Dec 05, 2014 ⬚
- Best news show on #EricGarner at: http://t.co/vi2qNYjlH7 #ICantBreathe #HandsUpDontShoot #HandsUpWalkout #BlackLivesMatter Dec 05, 2014 ⬚
- Cop vs officer? A Officer lives up to the oath to protect & serve. A cop does not; Kills people, is unjust, & this includes the silent ones Dec 05, 2014 ⬚
- Thanks @LeeGoldbergABC7 @MARS_ON_Spotify @ibr270 @letterstospam

@AlchemicJourney for being top new followers in my community this week Dec 05, 2014

- #Clinton backs #Obama call for task force on police. Are u kidding me? Out of touch. #icantbreathe http://t.co/CB9ZL1ngiv Dec 05, 2014
- Even the fox news crowd didn't defend the cops #EricGarner #HandsUpDontShoot #HandsUpWalkout ##icantbreathe http://t.co/W3pRm6wH1w Dec 05, 2014
- Mlk and Ghandi said there is no obligation to obey unjust or racist laws. #Icantbreathe #ericgarner #hands up walkout #blacklivesmatter Dec 05, 2014
- #EricGarner #cnn coverage #nyc http://t.co/eTtkRyaSBh Dec 05, 2014
- The #Ferguson march to the capital #HandsUpDontShoot http://t.co/yKWg7u2Fyr Dec 05, 2014
- Questions: why did guard do nothing in #Ferguson? http://t.co/guYwoGXavh Dec 05, 2014
- Where was the national guard during Ferguson fires and "looting" #Ferguson http://t.co/oHfrMMZ98j Dec 05, 2014
- Looks like a black man is killed every 28 hours by police in this country might not be an

exaggeration. #ICantBreathe #BlackLivesMatter Dec 05, 2014 ⚷

- Today White cop in Arizona kills unarmed black man. #ICantBreathe #EricGarner #HandsUpDontShoot #BlackLivesMatter http://t.co/0pxUCdRCzb Dec 05, 2014 ⚷

- Choke hold cop not indicted but man who took picture of it all was indicted. #icantbreathe #ericgarner http://t.co/OvktzMCb9s Dec 05, 2014 ⚷

- Behind closed doors: Republicans making plans to war on the poor & decrease taxes for the rich. They never let up. At: https://t.co/zmdqW86Xcj Dec 05, 2014 ⚷

- @2sense2 @EyedUsa Absolutely. I am just saying we got a backlog of cops. (smile) Dec 05, 2014 ⚷

- @EyedUsa @2sense2 If a looter breaks the law he should go to jail; so should cops KKK. Everybody. We all can agree on that? Dec 05, 2014 ⚷

- Well Santa Claus is going to be leaving a lot of lumps of coal in Christmas stockings in Washington DC. This year. #ICantBreathe Dec 05, 2014 ⚷

- I'm saying positively, for sure, absolutely, the last time I get sweet-talked by a politician angling for my vote. Always turns out bad. Dec 05, 2014 ⚷

- @EyedUsa Fox news. Saw their video, Yes definitely a mix but I saw whites, blacks & some other nationality. But note police did nothing! Why Dec 05, 2014
- @2sense2 @EyedUsa Well I would post if I had clips with blacks and whites. Humm,, I will have a look again. Dec 05, 2014
- Look folks even Charles Krauthammer and Glenn Beck came out against the #Ericgarner verdict. Who is to the right of Krauthammer? Dec 05, 2014
- @2sense2 @EyedUsa You would think there would be black guys in there somewhere. I didn't see any. Do have a clip with black guys in there? Dec 05, 2014
- Don't forget all the people out there that got arrested -480 of them. Do what you can to help. Don't forget them this season. #ICantBreathe Dec 05, 2014
- How is it calling 911 gets black children killed? #ICantBreathe Dec 05, 2014
- @victoriaramirez Love ya Dec 05, 2014
- #NYC quote: #ericgarner, who u going to believe, the NYPD or your lying eyes? Dec 05, 2014
- @lhmcelroy Still amazed. Even Charles Krauthammer and Glenn Beck condemned it. Dec 05, 2014
- Look I don't want to be political, I'm a writer by trade,16 books, but u can't walk by Hell while

people suffering, ignore it & by yr latte Dec 05, 2014

- What I am saying is this holiday season too many people of color in this country will be hanging black black crape Dec 05, 2014
- Hate to break the news but the clips I saw of #Ferguson :looters" had a lot of white guys coming out of those stores. Investigation? KKK? Dec 05, 2014
- @victoriaramirez @Jcnorthbranch I didn't. Dec 05, 2014
- How can all the "good cops" on NYPD keep silent? There must be one in the whole 5,000? #ICantBreathe The big blue wall of silence. Dec 05, 2014
- Here is article on Wisconsin independent investigation law: http://t.co/36U29pa8gc #ICantBreathe #Ferguson Dec 05, 2014
- #NYC quote: They penned us in like animals, gassed us, shouted for us to disperse all the while making sure we couldn't disperse. Cop crap Dec 05, 2014
- #NYC quote: "Had 500 people follow me today. Oh, wait. It the cops." #ICantBreathe #EricGarner #Ferguson Dec 05, 2014
- Wisconsin first state to require independent investigation of all deaths in police custody. 49 more states to go. #ICantBreathe #Ferguson Dec 04, 2014

- Here we have another example of the #NYPD allowed to get away with investigating itself What?. #ICantBreathe #Ferguson #HandsUpDontShoot Dec 04, 2014 ⌘
- Let me get this straight: I get killed cause I am selling single cigarettes? Dec 04, 2014 ⌘
- What I am starting to realize is that minorities and what is happening to them is just the tip of a spear that includes all of us. Dec 04, 2014 ⌘
- #Holocaust: Our Jewish brothers & sisters ought to understand that. Raise yr voices. #ICantBreathe #HandsUpDontShoot #HandsUpWalkout What? Dec 04, 2014 ⌘
- Voting suppression & rigging, an out of control police army, corrupt politicians, & finance system, joblessness, bad schools, war crazies. Dec 04, 2014 ⌘
- @NancyWonderful @Destroy_ALEC You are absolutely right Nancy. But we are years behind them in organization and money. Dec 04, 2014 ⌘
- What we have here is a holocaust for people of color. This can't be an accident. #ICantBreathe #Ferguson #HandsUp #BlackLivesMatter Dec 04, 2014 ⌘
- Not just men and boys of color: #Women of color are the fastest growing segment of the incarceration population. https://t.co/LuMJdzdJBX Dec 04, 2014 ⌘

- What's up with commissions? I want tanks & swat teams, tear gas, rubber bullets & trigger happy cops out of my neighborhood. It's that simple Dec 04, 2014 ᴁ
- Crimingwhilewhite http://t.co/bFgZ3V0gER Is there disparity in arrests for whites? Some whites say yes. Dec 04, 2014 ᴁ
- #NYC quote: "Terrorists world-wide are happy. They don't have to bring tanks & guns; steal ones Americans have in every neighborhood-Syria? Dec 04, 2014 ᴁ
- If cops dressed up like ham sandwiches, indictments would go up. True that. #ICantBreathe #Ferguson Dec 04, 2014 ᴁ
- #NYC quote: "None of us civilians have tanks & guns. So officers what is the tank for?" #ICantBreathe #HandsUpDontShoot #HandsUpWalkout Dec 04, 2014 ᴁ
- Famously judge once said any prosecutor can indict a "ham sandwich" if he wants to. So cops should be forced to dress up as ham sandwiches. Dec 04, 2014 ᴁ
- #DeBlasio's presidential hopes on the line in the #EricGarner situation. So far failing test. Might not even get re-elected. #ICantBreathe Dec 04, 2014 ᴁ
- @simonconroy You are so correct. Only when I started to really listen to my kids did I start to get educated. Dec 04, 2014 ᴁ

- @galeharrier Hey beautiful site! True Mary, not all of us. Dec 04, 2014 
- Link to article: chokehold officer a "model" http://t.co/ES8FaL2DIY #ICantBreathe Dec 04, 2014 
- Chokehold cop a "model" officer?. This is deliberately provocative cause cops know disruption is more overtime in their pockets-politics. Dec 04, 2014 
- No, no I am saying it is always the kids in each generation which wake up the adults. Adults get comfortable. Kids live in the real world. Dec 04, 2014 
- @hrw Yes Renee but people are waking up. We all are not alone now. Kids are waking us up. Dec 04, 2014 
- @AnastasiaYeager Humm, good point. I seem to remember only 1 years ago. But Cleveland is positively scary. Guy who shot Tamir evaluated "F" Dec 04, 2014 
- Sad fact: our white brothers & sisters have been quite happy to ignore what has gone on for years with the police. Now, they're seeing cost. Dec 04, 2014 
- Justice department finds Cleveland #PoliceBrutality guilty of "shocking brutality" #ICantBreathe at: http://t.co/7wu9rS5tvW Dec 04, 2014 
- I mean 70 % of our congress people & senators are millionaires & get rich from insider

trading info they get from being on committees. Dec 04, 2014

- You know USAToday has done nice work lately. See tweets below on disparities in arrests across the entire country. Interactive. Good work. Dec 04, 2014

- Thanks @wicked_cricket @3318082 @Anon_Solidarity @CarperJones @musikate for being top engaged members in my community this week Dec 04, 2014

- @Disciple4Lif Hey Michael, did an essay on Jesus. Love him. See at: http://t.co/10kmIWgd5P Dec 04, 2014

- @Disciple4Lif The kids out there are the future. "You" are those that think they are bums and thugs. Dec 04, 2014

- Report from the kitchen table: This is where hearts & minds get expanded, changed or hardened; where generations meet & the future decided Dec 04, 2014

- #NYC quote: "We aren't bums and thugs; we are the future and you are the past." #ICantBreathe Dec 04, 2014

- #NYC learned lesson: Don't be blinded by skin color black or white. Listen careful, reach out, make friends & dump impostors, #ICantBreathe Dec 04, 2014

- #NYC quote: "This country is run by two gangs which take turns shaking everybody down for votes and money." #ICantBreathe Dec 04, 2014

- @QueenPhillippa So true. But this generation is different on those points, Not so druggy, got a home with parents. Dec 04, 2014
- Used to be middle class kids were not able to relate to the poor they marched with. Class differences. MC kids now understand poverty better Dec 04, 2014
- The tax rate on the rich was 94%.1954 Prosperity country-wide. Today's rate: 37.5% corporate. Most don't pay that. 10% avg-less than u or I Dec 04, 2014
- #NYC protest quotes: "I should have to work a low wage job all my life so you can live in your penthouse?" #ICantBreathe Dec 04, 2014
- I mean we've created a whole underclass of low wage workers, indebted students, minorities, now starting to see they all have been screwed. Dec 04, 2014
- What's different from the 60's: we had jobs & income & could get in the streets, these young people don't & are very upset. They'll stick. Dec 04, 2014
- Fact: Power never gives up power willingly due to the power of yr logic have to threaten someone's job: stay in the streets to get action. Dec 04, 2014
- The 60's: That peace sign had a balled up fist behind it & resistance in the streets & longevity

The Montgomery Bus Boycott took a year. Dec 04, 2014

- @amin7e So true. Even I am shocked as I learn more. Dec 04, 2014
- @CRAZYONSI As i read history the Irish got out of poverty by becoming the cops in most cities. Was a way to middle class. Dec 04, 2014
- @CRAZYONSI Don't know Mike in US and worldwide people are fed up. Maybe u should encourage your white friends to get into the street. Dec 04, 2014
- Trust is not the issue-Cease & Desist is the Issue. Cameras can & are turned off. Cops-go to jail just like everybody else. #ICantBreathe Dec 04, 2014
- Where are our people of color leaders? Why aren't they calling for "tank the tanks" police reforms or real change? #ICantBreathe Dec 04, 2014
- The new-old apartheid: Get out of school: fines, warrants: hustle black-brown men straight to jail. 2.6m: most in the world #ICantBreathe Dec 04, 2014
- Well this is the wakeup call: it is really true: The color of your skin means nothing once u get into power. Lesson learned. #ICantBreathe Dec 04, 2014

- Apparently justice in this country comes in three colors: white, black, and officer blue. #ICantBreathe Dec 04, 2014 ⚐
- @CRAZYONSI sure are. Cops swat team whites too but whites get different treatment in the justice system. Dec 04, 2014 ⚐
- The numbers below r accurate. Google Us service deaths & police involved deaths. #Ican'tbreathe police death even low cause no records kept. Dec 04, 2014 ⚐
- 4,491 U.S. service members killed in Iraq between 2003 and 2014. Justifiable homicide killings=400 per year. Tot. 2003-14=4,400 #icantbreathe Dec 04, 2014 ⚐
- What I am saying is that the number of people killed through police violence equals the number of deaths we had in Iraq- 5k #icantbreathe Dec 04, 2014 ⚐
- Never any blame, never any shame, thousands dead. #ICantBreathe Dec 04, 2014 ⚐
- Well would u feel that way if u had to watch your son father brother get murdered on video choked to death & the guilty party then go free? Dec 04, 2014 ⚐
- How Would the U.S. Media Cover the Eric Garner Case If It Happened in Another Country? http://#ICantBreath http://t.co/dT9JqF3IQ0 via @slate Dec 04, 2014 ⚐

- Reaction
  #ICantBreathe http://t.co/tnpqEpw9e7 Dec 04, 2014 🖉
- #Police involved deaths: the history nyc
  #ICantBreathe http://t.co/Uugp3ktZlt Dec 04, 2014 🖉
- #Nytimes editorial
  #ICantBreathe http://t.co/ND2UQpM2Ej Dec 04, 2014 🖉
- Coverage of #EricGarner
  #ICantBreathe http://t.co/67eA8IDW47 Dec 04, 2014 🖉
- "Dystopia" #story #writing #novel #politics
  at: http://t.co/H7TE1yJX5e Dec 04, 2014 🖉
- "Oh my or my why do all our white brethren think that when the hammer comes down they will get a pass. Not." Dec 04, 2014 🖉
- Our white bros & sister just can't believe they are part of the "control the population" plan, still thinking privilege, but sorry no. U too Dec 04, 2014 🖉
- No, not all bad, it's got people having to deal with all this unconscious racial stuff, our job is to engage them, talk to them, feel them. Dec 04, 2014 🖉
- Remember, "You can't kill an idea" but damn they love trying. Dec 04, 2014 🖉
- U don't have to be right about everything, or even understand about everything, it is that u

understand all is part of our planetary journey Dec 04, 2014 ⚐

- It is not only the phony "you don't see color", it is that u don't" feel" color and can see a person soul. Then you enter the "human" realm Dec 04, 2014 ⚐
- All those that feel they are getting screwed by the present system-hands up. That's all you and we need to know. Join together. Dec 04, 2014 ⚐
- @PlatoCase Yo and Yo again. Dec 04, 2014 ⚐
- To be clear Bro. Skin color does not matter in matters of justice. Grow beyond skin color and you overcome injustice. Dec 04, 2014 ⚐
- Don't diss potential friends, comrades, collaborators, organizers cause of the color of their skin. That's dumb. Dec 04, 2014 ⚐
- The sad fact is that most whites know they are privileged over blacks & minorities & know they are members of the "club" & blacks aren't. Dec 04, 2014 ⚐
- What is galling is that we are paying for our own suppression via taxes. Dec 04, 2014 ⚐
- I have been told "u are our number 1 target, educated person of color. Got to bring you down." #Ferguson, #Handupwalkout #EricGarner Dec 04, 2014 ⚐
- I have been in jail cells with blacks & whites. The whites get picked up. The people of color

go to jail, & get a record. What's up? Dec 04, 2014

- Not just blacks; browns, women, young people of color around the world are revolting, fed up, had enough. #Ferguson, #EricGarner Dec 04, 2014
- Let's make this clear: In driving black neighborhoods u see 5 cops every hr. not cause of high crime it's because they can get high cash. Dec 04, 2014
- Am I scared around cops? Yes, guns, tanks, trigger happy, handcuffs, yeah. Has it happened to me? Yes. What about u? If not u just don't know Dec 04, 2014
- Don't have to be super-bright to smell rotten fish. #EricGarner #Ferguson #HandsUpDontShoot Dec 04, 2014
- Aliens? Sure. Some days just walking home I feel like I am surrounded by aliens in blue, with guns & an attitude. Every person of color does Dec 04, 2014
- #Ferguson quote" "Hey man what is the tank for?" Dec 04, 2014
- Sorry, but my feeling is that a good rant for justice, is just ginger-peachy. Dec 04, 2014
- Again I am saying even if he was found guilty, the taxpayers would still have to pay the 75m. That is not right either. We need a remedy here Dec 04, 2014

- Well, no where in the civilized world do you get the death penalty for selling loose cigarettes--especially since he was not that day anyway Dec 04, 2014
- Come to think of it if more police departments had to pay a % of lawsuits for misconduct, u can bet shootings would stop or drop like a rock Dec 04, 2014
- #EricGarner family to sue for 75m. I say whole police force should pay a % of that, not put it all on the taxpayers-it's done elsewhere. Dec 04, 2014
- Two deaths #Ferguson and #Icantbreathe two apologies. As if. Dec 04, 2014
- Well it seems clear that money and career come before morality for most police departments and politicians. No protection, not much serving. Dec 03, 2014
- Like the #Ferguson situation, the #EricGarner ruling has been greeting by dead silence by most of our leaders. What's up? Dec 03, 2014
- Well we could parse technicalities but a man is dead. Period. Coroner ruled it a homicide and I agree with that. #ICantBreathe Dec 03, 2014
- Well the NYC #Mayor and #Police Chief in NY made it clear chokeholds are banned, no matter what.
At: http://t.co/wgqPFVBql9 #ICantBreathe Dec 03, 2014

- Humm. True chokehold is banned to use on people and is considered "excessive force" and Garner's death is clear evidence of excessive force. Dec 03, 2014
- @MiddleClassPoli @VlanTrunk You're correct, just found out. Still the police policy says not to use it. Did see that DeBlasio supports it. Dec 03, 2014
- @ #EricGarner quote: "Why is it we have a concept of protesters rioting, but not a concept of police rioting?" Dec 03, 2014
- Scary to me is the wider implication that "no life matters if you get killed by a cop." Dec 03, 2014
- #EricGarner quote: "He was killed with an outlawed, illegal choke-hold and they still could not find anything that policeman was guilty of." Dec 03, 2014
- The #Guardian on the #EricGarner case: At: https://t.co/dLn8uzXltv Dec 03, 2014
- #EricGarner quote: "Urging citizens "to be calm"-a message that ought to be delivered to the police-the ones with the guns." #ICantBreathe Dec 03, 2014
- @alinatede Yes me too. But we have to get him to "Tank the Tanks" program. People getting killed behind it. Dec 03, 2014
- #Ferguson, #HandsUpDontShoot #HandsUpWalkout We have to get this military

equipment out of our towns and cities "Tank the Tanks" Dec 03, 2014 ⌖

- #Obama speech on #EricGarner #icantbreathe at:http://t.co/gQYKriV6kT Dec 03, 2014 ⌖
- We have to tell Congress to "Tank the Tanks" #Ferguson, #Handsupwalkout Dec 03, 2014 ⌖
- @RaeJean9 Gotta tell Obama to "tank the tanks" Dec 03, 2014 ⌖
- #NewsWeek Article: "How #America's Police Became an Army"
  at: http://t.co/GmEkYPcRmw Dec 03, 2014 ⌖
- Small towns get heavy #military gear too, one huge vehicle is parked in the barn in rural Indiana. See at: http://t.co/MPh5tmrcEm Dec 03, 2014 ⌖
- Even Stars and Stripes mag aimed at military questioned this militarization. http://t.co/Ahi8TNhQAn Hell this feels like an internal army. Dec 03, 2014 ⌖
- No, we don't have just the militarization of cops, we have the militarization of cities & town it's the whole country. http://t.co/vDrzdhrzoP Dec 03, 2014 ⌖
- Yes, elites have an interest in unrest; justifies more repression, more cops, more tanks, less civil rights, divides pop racially, 9-11. Dec 03, 2014 ⌖
- This kind of thing has happened in dozens of countries, We have to get smart & see it could

happen to us. We're becoming a banana republic Dec 03, 2014 ⌐

- Only hope is that somebody in government maybe the military will refuse to go along and refuse to carry out the plan. Dec 03, 2014 ⌐
- @ttank66 Scary indeed. There are evil people in the world and a lot of them live in Washington DC Dec 03, 2014 ⌐
- Yes, look at list of cities with tanks. It is white communities as well as minority communities. Tells you something. Dec 03, 2014 ⌐
- My thought? No this is not ultimately aimed at minorities, it is also aimed, in the end, at controlling the entire American population. Dec 03, 2014 ⌐
- Here we go again, no indictment, provoke reaction, divide country racially, send in troops, round people up, jail, fines, Marshall law. Dec 03, 2014 ⌐
- #Icantbreathe thanks Jennifer for the hash tag. Dec 03, 2014 ⌐
- @ttank66 @EddieGEastcoast Same agenda, divide the country racial, provoke rebellion, send in the troops, round people up, jail. Dec 03, 2014 ⌐
- #NYquotes coming thick & fast: "What is it going to take to make cops in this country accountable? How many deaths? #Ferguson #Hands #Garner Dec 03, 2014 ⌐

- Who is #EricGarner? Here is a link. #Ferguson #handsupwalkout
  At: http://t.co/v7HaoEWsOm Dec 03, 2014
- Another no indictment case? Does anyone think this is helpful? There are 4 lesser charges they could have ruled. Not even community service Dec 03, 2014
- No Grand Jury indictment in the Eric #Garner choke hold case. #Ferguson #handsupwalkout at: http://t.co/YEc433RQ7w Dec 03, 2014
- If I were a mystery #writer, I would look into the who & the why of the only fatality in the Ferguson situation. That story would go large. Dec 03, 2014
- Congress people: got their mouth taped shut with dollar bills, their ears plugged with propaganda, their eyes are closed, & they got a tick. Dec 03, 2014
- Taxpayers on the hook for 40 million dollar law suit in #Ferguson. Oh, when the lawyers get involved, stop empty your pockets, & bend over. Dec 03, 2014
- Yes, but it is stunning to me to see on the map below that over 1,500 counties in this country are WORSE than #Ferguson on racial arrests? Dec 03, 2014
- #Ferguson quote: "What to do from here? Ain't no swami, but I do know that killing, gassing, and tanking is the wrong way." Dec 03, 2014

- And, just because I disagree with that other someone does not give me the right to regard that someone as sub-human and harm them. Dec 03, 2014
- True, we all have biases & opinions. My point is simple: it takes courage to say to someone u disagree with, tell me more. Some can't do that Dec 03, 2014
- Here is article to go with chart below #Ferguson disparity in arrests exists nationwide. See at: http://t.co/EAWGMrtMCh Dec 03, 2014
- Does your county have a greater disparity of racial arrests than #Ferguson? See your state and your county at: http://t.co/9cV5ipmORv … Dec 03, 2014
- Occupy Wall Street volunteers defend #Ferguson protesters in court — RT USA http://t.co/OewQLyjEln Dec 03, 2014
- Here is two gun Pete: #Chicago http://t.co/yd1Br8m2Bg & https://t.co/4gdTUDW8Q1 Dec 03, 2014
- #Chicago? I had gang murder a friend in front of me, got bullet wound fragment from two gun Pete still in my leg, & more. Yes I know Chicago Dec 03, 2014
- @NLWeil @BlueDavidC I am wondering where they were and what role they had in kids death and fire. Need an investigation Dec 03, 2014

- Chicago & police force? I grew up there listening to family & community members telling of being picked up & beaten regularly. Going on yrs. Dec 03, 2014
- @NLWeil @BlueDavidC Found the letter: At: #KKK flyer promising "lethal force" in #Ferguson at: http://t.co/EMWZvJWjSE ... Dec 03, 2014
- #KKK flyer promising "lethal force" in #Ferguson at: http://t.co/m2dbLE1Y49 Dec 03, 2014
- True again. But what is and was shocking to me is some showing armed in #Ferguson seemed to want a shooting race war. Dec 03, 2014
- @NLWeil @BlueDavidC They made threats a letter and video. I have citation if you want to see it. Had ties to Ferguson police. Honest. Dec 03, 2014
- @NLWeil @BlueDavidC was a twin who was a friend of Brown. Maybe mistaken identity. Still no investigation. Dec 03, 2014
- Sad fact: 1.5m in cop and national guard, 40m in lawsuits for cop misconduct, county broke #Ferguson pop. to pay for their own mistreatment. Dec 03, 2014
- Where or where are our leaders? They all seem to be meeting behind closed doors figuring how they came avoid this whole #Ferguson thing? Dec 03, 2014

- If you are asking me to trust the Ferguson police and the wheels of justice, I am saying, don't think so. Dec 03, 2014
- #Ferguson: Murdered black man a key witness in the Brown killing & set on fire. Where is the investigation? http://t.co/mazDqlxLJ9 ... Dec 03, 2014
- The only killing-fatality in #Ferguson: black man, murdered and set on fire. Why was he killed, what did he know? Why no investigation? Dec 03, 2014
- Most empires in history fall because they squander money, taxes and personnel in external wars, and collapse or people revolt. Dec 03, 2014
- Here is the link to the NYC city billion in expenses over the 10 years. http://t.co/bSfWCXjqXD Dec 03, 2014
- Feel like the once #mlddle class is getting its bones picked by the rich who laugh investing our dollars in China. Dec 03, 2014
- More: Lawsuits cost #cities millions. In #NYC it cost one billion over 10 year period. Why. Who caused it, who paid? Dec 03, 2014
- Well simple as long as there's a whole generation of young people: no job, no future & living on food stamps & parents, they'll be upset. Dec 03, 2014
- Police misconduct 740m between 2006-2011. 99% of this paid for by taxpayers. Ferguson

likely 40m in costs.
See http://t.co/BQqCAXapAQ Dec 03, 2014 🖉

- @ttank66 Billion? Did cops have to pay any of that. Some cities do that. Dec 03, 2014 🖉
- Our Weekly #Newspaper. #United #Kingdom #Britain edition at: 12/2/14
  at: https://t.co/DmUrBC6SF3 Dec 03, 2014 🖉
- #Nytimes most notable #books of 2014.
  at: http://t.co/KEZb8pYCkP Dec 03, 2014 🖉
- #Police shootings cost cites millions:
  See: http://t.co/6LtF3xxDc2 Dec 03, 2014 🖉
- Don't miss any #Tweets. See them all #Ferguson, #HandsUpWalkout
  at: http://t.co/0NQCLhcy89 press "get tweets" to see them. Dec 02, 2014 🖉
- Here is the #Chicago #Police and #Torture #Genocide #UN action: at:
  #Ferguson https://t.co/Y91iDKZdLQ Dec 02, 2014 🖉
- UN committee claims torture by #Chicago #police & demands reparations. Electric and cattle prods used? #Ferguson
  at: http://t.co/uaSbTDunLO Dec 02, 2014 🖉
- The not-discussed killing: black man killed in his car then he was set on fire. Investigation? #HandsUpWalkout
  at: http://t.co/j9hAsIbmPH ... Dec 02, 2014 🖉
- What is wrong with war? Govt. borrows money to pay for it: War profiteers get rich and you & I

pay the debt. See: http://t.co/BvTIzFuv68 Dec
02, 2014 ☁

- The not-discussed killing in #Ferguson, black
  man killed in his car & then he was set on fire.
  Investigation? at: http://t.co/j9hAsIbmPH Dec
  02, 2014 ☁
- Gasoline headed for $2 dollars or less by
  Christmas? That's good and that's bad.
  At: http://t.co/UmrTUDPdUA Dec 02, 2014 ☁
- "The Street" ranks the 10 "dumbest" #states in
  the US. Wow at: http://t.co/WecfYl3MsB Dec
  02, 2014 ☁
- 10 most crime ridden states? Mostly rural
  states, not big city states, mostly white pop.
  states, mostly gun
  states. http://t.co/X9sSiTYQyA Dec 02, 2014 ☁
- #Ferguson sign; "Got to be blind not to c
  something moving close to yr face, got to be
  numb not to feel something moving under you-
  a new day Dec 02, 2014 ☁
- #NYtimes, #Ferguson, #Handsupwalkout,
  Protests continue nationwide. Incredible photos
  At: http://t.co/OlsCYuWp4G Dec 02, 2014 ☁
- Time? Now is the time: What? Organize: Why?
  The planet is dying. How: Write, call, talk,
  demand, and get ready to act and then
  act. Dec 02, 2014 ☁
- 10 billion to one odds: Parent saying to
  teenage daughter "You are not having enough

- sex: and US govt official saying ok, we have been lying Dec 02, 2014 ⏎
- Biggest mistake humans have made on planet? Aside from greed & power it's forgetting that animals, plants r fellow travelers on this planet. Dec 02, 2014 ⏎
- To activate maps below click on a state & then you can see individual counties. These are FBI figures. My stars. #Ferguson #HandsUpWalkout Dec 02, 2014 ⏎
- Mind you chart below is 'worse" than #Ferguson and includes hundreds of police departments across this nation. This is a nation-wide issue. Dec 02, 2014 ⏎
- Does your county have a greater disparity of racial arrests than Ferguson? See your state and your county at: http://t.co/9cV5ipmORv ... Dec 02, 2014 ⏎
- Well I am just saying why is it so hard to say "You can't continue to kill people, claiming that you were "scared" #Ferguson Dec 02, 2014 ⏎
- #Ferguson protestors say #Obama white house meeting not enough. Will stay in the streets. #HandsUpWalkout http://t.co/tQ7TYiKnUU Dec 02, 2014 ⏎
- When White People Riot. They do all the time more than blacks? #Ferguson at: http://t.co/VAqTkj1vuL ... Dec 02, 2014 ⏎

- #Prostitution, #Sex Workers and the Great #Recession. The Economist looks at market trends. What is going on?
  At: http://t.co/42zYFxH9Tn] Dec 02, 2014 🗗
- #Obama says "trust" essential between police & community. Really? Trust is not what you want. You want "cease and desist" Trust comes later. Dec 02, 2014 🗗
- Being awake is realizing we have a system that every dime we make we put into a bank where it goes directly to govt, every dime-in 24 hrs. Dec 02, 2014 🗗
- @burberryant true. What is so sad is that our money is financing them. Dec 02, 2014 🗗
- Conspiracy? Hate to break it to you, but government IS an organized conspiracy. Dec 02, 2014 🗗
- Hell Americans in history have always rebelled when they have had enough, whiskey, ww1 vets, 100's times. Govt power always oversteps Dec 02, 2014 🗗
- Ok, Mary, Yes faith is nice to have, and I do put my faith in the higher powers, but with today's govt. I am putting on my cynical garb. Dec 02, 2014 🗗
- Yes, spent years wondering don't they know what is happening out here with real people? Scary answer yes they do, & have made their own plans Dec 02, 2014 🗗

- If u want to understand r current govt. u have to learn to think like they do. They have given up on us, looking out now solely 4 themselves Dec 02, 2014 ₪
- Yes #Ferguson did get rid of Darren Wilson, no severance, no pension. Out the door, Cost them 1.5 million & he got rich. Dec 02, 2014 ₪
- Am I paranoid? I'm warming up to it. Dec 02, 2014 ₪
- Well you have a point. What i am trying to say is that fear is the major cause of blindness in political matters. Dec 02, 2014 ₪
- What I am saying: the US government is spending one trillion dollars of our money a year figuring out how to control us Americans. Seriously Dec 02, 2014 ₪
- Bottom line is the so many people in this country are faced with work for "security-military-govt dominators, or starve. Need another choice Dec 02, 2014 ₪
- Government has become a street-level magician, never look at the hand they are putting forth, look at the other hand they are hiding. Dec 02, 2014 ₪
- The promise to restore order, protect property, punish specific groups, protect our women, is the message of every fascist group in history. Dec 02, 2014 ₪
- Sad commentary on #Ferguson Darren Wilson gets half a million, paid interviews & city gets

1.5 million bill. No wonder they forced him out. Dec 02, 2014 🔗

- It is a win-win for military control. Create conditions for rebellion, if the pop. accepts control great. If they rebel, more troops-win-win Dec 02, 2014 🔗
- No, I'm saying that if u want an excuse for more control & oppression, you have an interest in creating the conditions which spark rebellion Dec 02, 2014 🔗
- The US is doing in the cities exactly the same thing it does in countries around the world. Create chaos & division and then militarize. Dec 02, 2014 🔗
- Gangs, in the United States love the militarization of police policy. Big armor comes to my hood-just 4 the for taking. Stuff will disappear Dec 02, 2014 🔗
- The silence on militarization of police? Each group secretly thinks this military power will only used against minorities. Not. #Ferguson Dec 02, 2014 🔗
- If i was paranoid: the militarization of police is deliberate policy of population control on a mass scale. Dec 02, 2014 🔗
- So sad the Obama administration will continue to supply military equipment to police to fight "terrorism" Lots of those in #Ferguson? Scary. Dec 02, 2014 🔗

- Are we causing our own extinction? Looks like it. #Climate change http://t.co/zOf6G9V7xb Dec 02, 2014

- Half, repeat 50% of #British #police chiefs accused of corruption and improprieties. See at: http://t.co/hDEikvTAqR Dec 02, 2014

- Idea: charge entire police force part of the legal settlements in cop shootings. Happening now in some cities #Ferguson http://t.co/udBo93iUiQ Dec 02, 2014

- Well Mary, if money talks in our society, lets have it talk to the police just like it talks to the rest of us Dec 02, 2014

- @MRHRoberts huh. In Ferguson & many small towns fines on blacks, warrants, bail, give that small town 2.6 m per year, plus taxes. Who pays? Dec 02, 2014

- Let's face it folks white cops ain't doing such a great job in policing black communities Give black officers a chance. See if crime goes down Dec 02, 2014

- Idea is charge entire police force part of the huge legal settlements in cop shootings. Happening now is some cities http://t.co/cTHkkxVyRq … Dec 02, 2014

- Hate to be cynical: my police friends tell me that police like high black crime rates & stoking the fear that blacks will attack whites. Not Dec 02, 2014

- Put some community sensitive cops in Ferguson, watch the crime rate go down. This is proven "community policing model" some police are using Dec 02, 2014
- @Bureaucracybust Give black cops the same money and watch the crime rate go down. Will that happen you think? White cops doing a great job? Dec 02, 2014
- All I am saying that if cops and their comrades had to pay a portion of their salaries for shootings, shootings would go way down. @Ferguson Dec 02, 2014
- #Ferguson quote: We are paying the cops & they are shooting our kids? They fine us; get a shiny new cop HQ & "Justice" building we paid for? Dec 02, 2014
- The point Is that if u are a cop & go out and shoot someone, accidentally or or purpose why should I as the tax payer foot all of the bill? Dec 02, 2014
- The point is that with legal costs to cities at 3-6 million per year, who pays that money? Us taxpayers. Should cops pay a portion of that? Dec 02, 2014
- Data on cop involved shootings and arrests: http://t.co/U8E288aPKg Police shootings cost taxpayer millions per year http://t.co/6LtF3xxDc2 Dec 02, 2014

- Citizens 8 times more likely to be killed by cops than a terrorist:=amt killed in Iraq almost See: http://t.co/EzTCABejRC Dec 02, 2014
- U never know what is going to happen in life. Who'd have guessed that a mixed race Kenyan-White couple would produce a president? No one. Dec 02, 2014
- Well, my view, if you don't want to talk to people u disagree with, u are part of the problem and lack courage. Dialogue is for the sincere. Dec 02, 2014
- @9870513 Charging cops is already happening. See article. Dec 02, 2014
- @9870513 Humm, I like that one too. Money talks can work many different ways. Dec 01, 2014
- @Lightningrattle Yes, afraid of alienating their wall street funders. Dec 01, 2014
- Idea is charge entire police force a part of the huge legal settlements in cop shootings. Happening now is some cities http://t.co/cTHkkxVyRq Dec 01, 2014

The not-discussed killing: black man killed in his car then he was set on fire. Investigation? #HandsUpWalkout at: http://t.co/j9hAsIbmPH …

- 10 most crime ridden states? Mostly rural states, not big city states, mostly white pop.

states, mostly gun
states. http://t.co/X9sSiTYQyA Dec 02, 2014 ⮹

- #NYtimes, #Ferguson, #Handsupwalkout,
  Protests continue nationwide. Incredible photos
  At: http://t.co/OlsCYuWp4G Dec 02, 2014 ⮹

- Does your county have a greater disparity of
  racial arrests than Ferguson? See your state
  and your county
  at: http://t.co/9cV5ipmORv ... Dec 02, 2014 ⮹

- #Ferguson protestors say #Obama white
  house meeting not enough. Will stay in the
  streets.
  #HandsUpWalkout http://t.co/tQ7TYiKnUU Dec
  02, 2014 ⮹

- When White People Riot. They do all the time
  more than blacks? #Ferguson
  at: http://t.co/VAqTkj1vuL ... Dec 02, 2014 ⮹

- Idea is charge entire police force part of the
  huge legal settlements in cop shootings.
  Happening now is some
  cities http://t.co/cTHkkxVyRq ... Dec 02, 2014
  ⮹

- Data on cop involved shootings and
  arrests: http://t.co/U8E288aPKg Police

shootings cost taxpayer millions per year http://t.co/6LtF3xxDc2 Dec 02, 2014 🔗

- Citizens 8 times more likely to be killed by cops than a terrorist:=amt killed in Iraq almost See: http://t.co/EzTCABejRC Dec 02, 2014 🔗

- Idea is charge entire police force a part of the huge legal settlements in cop shootings. Happening now is some cities http://t.co/cTHkkxVyRq Dec 01, 2014 🔗

- The Obama plan in the wake of Ferguson? At: http://t.co/cTHkkxVyRq Dec 01, 2014 🔗

- 

- 30 cities: hundreds of schools participate in #Ferguson #HandsUpWalkout photos at: http://t.co/hlXdPKlHmp Dec 01, 2014 🔗

- #Ferguson #HandUpWalkOut spread all across the country at: http://t.co/4yp5eyluVR Dec 01, 2014 🔗

- Bystander looking at kids walking by in NY #HandsUpWalkout saying. Who are these kids? Answer came back: "They are our future." Dec 01, 2014 🔗

- #HandsUpWalkout NY had fifty schools participate. #Ferguson Photos at: https://t.co/Jwfqwhr6qp Dec 01, 2014 🔗

- Thanks .nhdogmom .litfests .winn1_winn .shaindelr for being top engaged members in my community this week (via http://t.co/O3OmZ7qX9H) Dec 01, 2014 🔗
- #HandsUpWalkout times for various cities: #Ferguson https://t.co/y9Hul2mh5m Dec 01, 2014 🔗
- #HandsUpWalkout the school walk out is happening today at: #Ferguson https://t.co/ang66w8Q6r ... Dec 01, 2014 🔗

- Sorry I love this photo. Again. White Cop-Black Kid hug in #Ferguson demonstration http://t.co/Vbf0Ksnh7f ... ... Community-one hug at a time. Dec 01, 2014 🔗
- Anyone think #Ferguson rioters are representative of all black people but the Austin shooter is not representative of white people? jrehling Dec 01, 2014 🔗
- People ask often what is "institutionalized racism" One word example: #Ferguson Dec 01, 2014 🔗
- Getting the population so poor that they have to work for slave wages and handouts from the government is not freedom nor democracy." Dec 01, 2014 🔗
- 3,000 of my #tweets (last year). Fixed link problem. All #Ferguson tweets Good thing is

tweets are all live!
At: http://t.co/jD0vQeVmhO ... Dec 01, 2014 ⊡

- A week after the #Ferguson decision: U can count on one hand how many of our Washington "leaders" who have spoken out. Where are you folks? Dec 01, 2014 ⊡
- Funny on the web: "Easy to tell who served on the #Ferguson grand jury. Look for the ones with the extraordinarily long noses" Dec 01, 2014 ⊡
- Check out .Krhawkins5's Tweet: https://t.co/dFtxuq2PwD Dec 01, 2014 ⊡
- Thanks .RAZRteam .Tropakana .suckit .MachinesPicks for being top new followers in my community this week (insight by http://t.co/2Cens2PdoL) Dec 01, 2014 ⊡
- That strange #Ferguson grand jury http://t.co/oUSB4XnbzU Dec 01, 2014 ⊡
- Ferguson quote: They make me & my kids pledge alliance to America everyday while the big companies betray US & us sending our jobs overseas Dec 01, 2014 ⊡
- Our weekly newspaper: #Ferguson. 80 of u contributed to this 12-1-14 edition. At: http://t.co/jRtZfnEKnd Dec 01, 2014 ⊡
- #Ferguson: Well the questions mount: Who burned memorial down, who burned church, who killed key witness, who torched stores. Do we know? Dec 01, 2014 ⊡

- Who burned Mike Brown's Church to the
  ground? #Ferguson
  At: http://t.co/oTb42wKRCP Dec 01, 2014 &

#Ferguson quote: We had KKK here looking for a
race war, Oathkeepers, crazies,out of towners, off
duty troopers & they blame us for violence Nov 30,
2014 &

Ferguson quote: "I am outside my house & he
screams "get down on the sidewalk." I didn't move
fast enough: resisting arrest-jail, fines." Nov 30, 2014
&
The #National #Bar #Association questions the
#Ferguson #Grand Jury Decision in #NYTimes
at: http://t.co/yO2LX3q6Z0 Nov 30, 2014 &

UN panel slams US on police brutality.
#Ferguson http://t.co/4ex69LQKAJ Nov 30, 2014 &
Notice how all of our so-called leaders in Washington
and elsewhere are terrified and silent on #Ferguson?
Where are u folks? Nov 30, 2014 &
3,000 of my #tweets (last year). Fixed link problem.
Good thing is tweets are all live!
At: http://t.co/jD0vQeVmhO Nov 30, 2014 &

Vets come home, no health care, dissed, no job; no
money, broken families , empty tributes don't make
things better, be a cop, security? Nov 30, 2014 &
It's not complicated. Sharing the wealth is more fair,
keeps the peace and avoids bloodshed in
societies. Nov 30, 2014 &

#Ferguson protestors lead #Time Magazine's
Balloting for "Person of the Year"

at: http://t.co/4EcpjGDpeQ Nov 30, 2014 ⬠ #Duke University Study of #Racism without #Racists. What is that? # Ferguson http://t.co/aLyoi0106b Nov 30, 2014 ⬠

Emotional hug between white cop and black kid goes viral #Ferguson at: http://t.co/AWmzPZY91J Nov 30, 2014 ⬠

The #WashingtonPost talks about White Privilege? # Ferguson Yep. At:http://t.co/6iqlA7Uqpf Nov 30, 2014 ⬠

Protesters march to governor's mansion; Darren Wilson Resigns:#Ferguson At: http://t.co/CLXUoSYrww Nov 30, 2014 ⬠

The American Dream is a nightmare for those trying to support their families this holiday season. .2nd mortgage, savings depleted, no job. Nov 29, 2014 ⬠
Here is the list of the 10 most hated: at: http://t.co/XFdETC2ddo Nov 29, 2014 ⬠

Getting the population so poor that they have to work for slave wages and handouts from the government is not freedom nor democracy." Nov 29, 2014 ⬠
What I object to is being lied to & more 2.7t dollars of tax payer money is missing ea. year-and they tell us "National Security". What? Nov 29, 2014 ⬠

"Well I am not the first one to suspect that politicians lie, that institutions cheat, don't listen to voters. I am not the only one." Nov 29, 2014 ⬠

"Truly, what is shocking to realize is that everything you see & hear: TV, Radio, Media, Movies, News, Sports is designed to propagandize u. Nov 29, 2014 ⬠

In 2010: 162,000 cases & only 11 of these resulted in no indictment. So #Ferguson failure to indict was very rare. http://t.co/fYc8AJs6VZ Nov 29, 2014 ₪

"The more money involved in institutions the more the lie becomes accepted as the truth." Nov 29, 2014 ₪

Actually yes. I do have my #Tweets going back to Dec 2013. Press "Get My Tweets" to see http://t.co/E5FTy94k4d you go http://t.co/jD0vQeVmhO Nov 29, 2014 ₪

#Tweets on #Twitter; Over the last 2 Years: at: http://t.co/Mw4fz1KdS6 Nov 29, 2014 ₪

Well I saying that the police, the military, FEMA, the Feds, CIA, FBI, seem to be all working toward one goal: control of the population. Nov 29, 2014 ₪

Well I wouldn't trust #FEMA to come to your aid in a crisis: they are practicing law enforcement techniques & crowd control, See ur manual Nov 29, 2014 ₪

Bring wall street down: Don't put your money in wall street banks; create local money clubs, stop giving them your 401k & paycheck ea. mo. Nov 29, 2014 ₪

"The biggest illusions: If I keep low they will pass me by: if I cooperate they will favor me, not them, If I join them they will protect me Nov 29, 2014 ₪

#Ferguson '#Black lives matter': Clashes as thousands of #Londoners protest police racism (VIDEO) — RT UK http://t.co/UYDOIsmzPa Nov 29, 2014 ₪

Fourth Day #Ferguson: 15
arrests http://t.co/t6C9LFPns9 Nov 29, 2014 ⬚

400 #Ferguson protesters arrested across US, unrest
persists — RT USA http://t.co/668BjRqAvp Nov 29,
2014 ⬚

Give the #gift of #knowledge & #information this year.
16 #books. $2 ea. Then email free copies to friends.
At: https://t.co/j0ulElim7h Nov 29, 2014 ⬚

The #History of #Human #Societies pt. 1: #Freedom
Struggles: http://t.co/1nlmgWNRda & pt.
2 http://t.co/KFfjdh9M7p Nov 29, 2014 ⬚
#Psychopaths in power. #psychology #psychiatry
#politics #business #police
at: http://t.co/u6uj60XVtt Nov 29, 2014 ⬚

Well, here is are the #books, the #essays, and the
#poetry all in one spot.
At: http://t.co/cVovRMSCKl Nov 29, 2014 ⬚

.tk69foryou Bounce off me, stick on you. (: Nov 29,
2014 ⬚

People ask often what is "institutionalized racism"
One word example: #Ferguson Nov 28, 2014 ⬚

No, seriously: I have a BA. MA. MBA and ETBTD: the
last two from Cal Berkeley. My Bio
at: http://t.co/cVovRMSCKl Nov 28, 2014 ⬚

"Don't have to be super-smart to know right from
wrong." Nov 28, 2014 ⬚

My background? I have two-three degrees but have

spent years having to unlearn that crap. Nov 28, 2014 ⊡

#Ferguson quote: These people's hearts are in their wallets and even then the last time they pulled that heart out was before slavery times. Nov 28, 2014 ⊡

Anyone think #Ferguson rioters are representative of all black people but the Austin shooter is not representative of white people? jrehling Nov 28, 2014 ⊡

#Ferguson quote: Look, to me it is not ok to kill an unarmed teenager, claiming you were "afraid." Nov 28, 2014 ⊡

#RussellBrand speaks on #Ferguson. At: http://t.co/oCl8ixOpVu Nov 28, 2014 ⊡

Media Coverage of #Ferguson at: Media ignoring peaceful Ferguson protests across the country: http://t.co/e91GsnqHes via .YouTube Nov 28, 2014 ⊡

www.ingramcontent.com/pod-product-compliance
Lightning Source LLC
Chambersburg PA
CBHW071345280526
45787CB00001B/227